# Pursuing God *in the* Quiet Places

## KAROL LADD

HARVEST HOUSE PUBLISHERS

EUGENE, OREGON

*Cover by Koechel Peterson & Associates, Inc., Minneapolis, Minnesota*

*Cover photo © Jupiterimages/Photos.com/Thinkstock*

*Back-cover author photo by Shooting Starr Photography, Cindi Starr, www.shootingstarrphotos.com*

**PURSUING GOD IN THE QUIET PLACES**
Copyright © 2011 by Karol Ladd
Published by Harvest House Publishers
Eugene, Oregon 97402
www.harvesthousepublishers.com

ISBN 978-0-7369-4629-2 (Padded Hardcover)
ISBN 978-0-7369-4630-8 (eBook)

**Printed in China**

11  12  13  14  15  16  17  18  19  / RDS-SK /  10  9  8  7  6  5  4  3  2  1

*Introduction*

# Knowing Him

*We can never know who or what we are till*
*we know at least something of what God is.*

A.W. TOZER

God wants us to know Him. Not just know about
Him, but to really know Him. What is He like?
What are His attributes? How does He interact with
us? These are questions tucked away in our hearts and
minds, and they often surface, especially when we go
through a challenge or difficulty. But how do we discover the answers to these questions?

More often than not, getting to know God takes
place in the quiet moments of our lives as we engage
His Word.

The Bible offers an open invitation to know and
understand who God is and how He works in our lives.
Granted, in the midst of our busy lives it is often difficult to find quiet moments to ponder His Word and
enjoy His presence. It is my hope that this book will
entice you to be intentional about creating a little cor-
ner of stillness in your life in order to know and understand God in a more intimate way.

The prophet Jeremiah revealed God's desire for His people to know and understand Him when he wrote,

> "Let not the wise boast of their wisdom
> or the strong boast of their strength
> or the rich boast of their riches,
> but let the one who boasts boast about this:
> that they have the understanding to know me,
> that I am the LORD, who exercises kindness,
> justice and righteousness on earth,
> for in these I delight,"
> declares the LORD.[1]

*Pursuing God in the Quiet Places* is designed to help you discover important truths about our heavenly Father. Beginning in Genesis and ending in Revelation, we will look at specific passages of Scripture that show us and teach us about God's nature. I believe your heart will overflow with a greater love for Him as a result of knowing Him and understanding His ways. May this devotional be a joyful part of the process.

*Karol Ladd*
*May 2011*

# Creator

*In the beginning God created
the heavens and the earth.*

Genesis 1:1

God is the Originator, the Designer, the Artist, and the Sustainer of all there is in heaven and on earth. We can see His creative strokes in every part of creation. The beauty of a sunset, the magnificence of the stars, the delicate details of a butterfly, the whimsical acts of a monkey, all point to a glorious hand that made them all. You too were fashioned and designed by our wonderful Creator. You are a masterpiece. Just as an artist delights in his masterpiece, so the Lord delights in you.

Our Designer knew exactly what He was doing when He formed the intricate details of our bodies. Every cell is coded with instructions as to how it should function within the body. From the smallest of details in an atom to the grandest of galaxies in the universe, all He has done inspires us with awe. Let us lift up our hearts in praise to the Almighty God, Creator of all. His magnificent work points to His power and beauty.

*He...*

# Spoke... and There Was

*God said, "Let there be light," and there was light.*
GENESIS 1:3

What power, what authority! God spoke and it happened. It's impossible to comprehend that from nothing came something. Every molecule in creation fell in line at the sound of His voice. He spoke and there was light. He spoke and there was a great expanse between the waters. He spoke and dry ground appeared. He spoke and there was the sun, along with the moon and the stars. He spoke and there were birds and fish and animals.

Everything came into being by Him and for Him. He is before all things, and by Him all things exist. Creation was not simply a random event. God deliberately orchestrated it. He is both the composer and conductor of the great symphony of life, written in His divine wisdom and carried out by His voice. His voice is immeasurably powerful in creation, and yet lovingly gentle as He speaks to our hearts. Are you listening for His voice?

*He...*

# Created Us in His Image

*God said, "Let us make man in our image, in our likeness."*
**GENESIS 1:27**

After God created all the birds and fish and every kind of animal according to its own kind, there was still one creature He had in mind. This one would be different from the others. This creature would bear His image. Humans are not created exactly like God, for an image is simply a reflection, not an exact replica of the model. We reflect certain characteristics about God, which separates us from plants, animals, birds, and fish.

What are those characteristics? We demonstrate His nature in our ability to reason, in our creativity and imagination, and in our speech. His character is reflected in our capacity to love, to forgive, to show patience and kindness toward one another. Just as He is an eternal being, He has given us an eternal soul that will continue when our bodies have long since decayed.

There is dignity and worth in every human, because each human is created in God's image. Let us recognize the value of every life including our own, for we reflect the image of our Creator.

*He...*

# Saw That Creation Was Very Good

*God saw all that he had made, and it was very good.*

Genesis 1:31

Have you ever watched an artist at work? Typically they will toil over their work for a while, then step back and observe it from several different angles, make some adjustments, and proceed with their work until the piece is finished. When God looked at all He created, He declared it was very good and rested from His work. The Grand Designer and Artist of all things created a glorious masterpiece that no artist on this earth can ever think of duplicating.

The word for "good" means "favorable; pleasing, right, best." God appraised each of the six days of creation, acknowledging that it was "good," but upon completion of everything He declared it all "very good." Creator and critic, He knew what He had created was the best. Let us live each day in appreciation of His creation. See the beauty in each person. Enjoy the pleasant surroundings in nature and stand in awe at the wonders of the universe. He made it all, and it is pleasing and wonderful. It is very good!

*He...*

# Rested

*On the seventh day he rested from all his work.*

GENESIS 2:2

The Bible tells us God does not slumber or sleep. If He does not grow weary or slumber, what does it mean that He "rested"? It means that He ceased from His work. He deliberately stopped and set aside the work of creation. He chose to establish the seventh day as a holy day, a day of Sabbath rest. The word *Sabbath* means "intermission or repose from labor." The Sabbath was a covenant sign of God's lordship over creation. The Israelites were instructed to observe a Sabbath rest, thereby identifying themselves as God's redeemed people.

God wanted His people to be set apart and be different than the rest of the world by ceasing from work one day a week. When we take a break from activity it gives us time to reflect on His goodness and trust Him for our provision. It also allows us to mentally and physically recoup from our work.

*Thank You, Father, for You know what is best for us. Thank You, Father, for establishing a pattern of rest for us.*

*He...*

# Walks with Us

*Enoch walked faithfully with God.*
GENESIS 5:23

When we walk with someone, we enjoy fellowship with them as we travel together. We have a choice to walk with God in a close relationship, or we can choose to wander in our own direction, doing as we please. Enoch chose to walk with God. Additionally, the Bible tells us that "Noah was a righteous man, the only blameless person living on earth at the time, and he walked in close fellowship with God."[2] Even in the Garden of Eden we see a mention of God's walking as we read, "The man and his wife heard the sound of the LORD God as he was walking in the garden in the cool of the day."

Paul wrote that just as we have received Christ Jesus as Lord, we are also to "walk in Him."[3] We can walk with God as we pray to Him throughout our day. It's one thing to know God as an acquaintance we simply see on Sundays. It's another thing to walk with Him in close fellowship. God invites us to walk with Him. Will you accept the invitation?

*He Was...*

# Heartbroken

*The LORD was sorry he had ever made them*
*and put them on the earth. It broke his heart.*
GENESIS 6:6 NLT

The extent of human wickedness had become so vast that the Bible says, "Everything they thought or imagined was consistently and totally evil."[4] So terrible was the evil intent of people's hearts that God came to the point of regretting He had made them and put them on the earth! Like a lover deeply hurt by his beloved, so the Lord's heart was broken. He had created man to fellowship with Him, to walk with Him, and to glorify Him, yet man turned away from God and went toward evil instead.

It's hard to imagine that God's heart could be broken, but it was. He loves us so very much that He doesn't want evil to come between us. He knows that evil only serves to kill and destroy. Yet His goodness and faithfulness enriches us and brings us life. Why would we turn from such a loving God?

*Father, hold us close to You and do not let us stray.*

*He Is a...*

# Covenant-Maker

*This is the sign of the covenant I am making...*
*I have set my rainbow in the clouds.*

**GENESIS 9:12-13**

The Almighty God has no obligation or legal commitment to make a covenant with mankind, yet He chose to give reassurance through an agreement with Noah that would last throughout all generations. He told Noah, "Never again will all life be destroyed by the waters of a flood; never again will there be a flood to destroy the earth."

He placed a rainbow in the clouds as a sign of this covenant. The Bible actually says that He put it there as a reminder. The beautiful rainbow serves as a reminder to us of His covenant, but it also is a reminder to God. He said that when He brings clouds and sees the rainbow, He will remember His covenant. We know that with a single word He could bring a flood to destroy all the earth, but He refrains. His rainbow serves as a sign of His mercy and grace toward mankind.

*He...*

# Speaks to His People

*The Lord had said to Abram,*
*"Go from your country...to the land I will show you."*
**Genesis 12:1**

God is not a silent god; He is a God who speaks. In the Old Testament He spoke to His people through prophets and through visions, and sometimes He spoke directly to His servants. He spoke to Abraham, Moses, Joshua, Daniel, Isaiah, and Jeremiah to name a few. Does God still speak to His people today?

One of the foundational ways He speaks to us is through His written Word, the Bible. We learn who God is and how He wants us to live as we read His Word. He also speaks through that still small voice, His Spirit within us, gently convicting us to turn from sin and lovingly prompting us to follow His direction.

Now we must be careful not to think that every thought we have is from Him. We must test it against Scripture. The more we get to know Him through Scripture, the more we recognize His voice.

*Father, open our ears to hear and our hearts to understand.*

*He...*

# Blesses

*I will make you into a great nation,*
*and I will bless you.*
GENESIS 12:2

God not only blesses us, but He blesses us for a purpose. He blesses us so we will be a blessing. The word *bless* means "to benefit." It implies abundantly or greatly. God blessed Abraham abundantly by building a great nation through his seed. He made Abraham's name great. God's blessings are different toward each one of us. Sometimes our blessings may come through the most difficult of trials. The purest gold comes through the most intense heat, and the most beautiful gems are formed through immense pressure.

Each one of us can look at ways God has blessed our lives. Are you focusing on the blessings He has given you, or are you focusing on the frustrations? Thank Him every day for the wonderful and unique ways He is blessing you, and then be diligent to use your blessings to bless the world around you.

# Most High—El Elyon

*Melchizedek king of Salem…*
*was priest of God Most High, and he blessed Abram.*
GENESIS 14:18-19

This mysterious Melchizedek, king of Salem, was the "priest of God Most High." We don't know much about Melchizedek, but one thing we do know is that he honored the God of Abram and worshipped Him as the High King of heaven, Creator of all. He gave a blessing to Abram, saying, "Blessed be Abram by God Most High, Creator of heaven and earth." The Hebrew word for God Most High is *El Elyon*, which designates God as the sovereign ruler over all the universe. This is a powerful name to know and understand, for it indicates that God is in control of all things. Nothing is outside of His reach.

Sovereignty characterizes the essence of who God is. Nothing lies outside the scope of His power and ability. Rulers and kings are not in control of this world—God is. Nothing happens without His permission. When we recognize His sovereignty as God Most High, it changes the way we view our circumstances. We trust more, and worry less.

# Great Reward

*Do not be afraid....*
*I am your shield,*
*your very great reward.*

**GENESIS 15:1**

God is not only our shield, He is also our very great reward. Notice that He did not say He would give Abram a very great reward—rather, *He* is the great reward. Those who know Him and abide with Him have the most wonderful blessing, the great reward of the God of all creation participating in their lives.

What more could we want? What greater reward could there be than experiencing a love relationship with the Lord God, who is the creator of the heavens and the Earth? We are rich indeed when we recognize that we have received the greatest reward in all eternity. The Lord God is our reward! His Spirit dwells with us. He is our shield. We do not need to be afraid, for He is all we need.

*Father, in You we have the greatest reward man can ever receive—Your presence in our lives through Your Spirit within us. Thank You.*

# Sees Our Pain

*You are the God who sees me...*
*I have now seen the One who sees me.*

GENESIS 16:13

When you feel as though no one knows the depth of your pain, remember that there is One who sees. You are not alone, for God sees you and knows your needs. In Genesis we read how God's angel met Hagar in the desert when she fled from the cruelty of Sarah. God meets us where we are and gently cares for our needs as well. We can rest assured that He sees our pain and challenges, and He understands.

We are not invisible to God. Just as Hagar was comforted by Him, so we can find our comfort in knowing that He sees all. It's easy to think that when bad things happen, He doesn't see our situation or care about our problems. Be patient. Wait on Him. Have faith in the God who sees and has a plan that is bigger and more enduring than we can imagine.

# God Almighty

*I am God Almighty; walk before me
faithfully and be blameless.*

GENESIS 17:1

The word "Almighty" is the Hebrew term *Shaddai*. In this word we sense the riches of God's grace and all-sufficient power. He lavishes His grace and mercy on His people. His supply is inexhaustible and bountiful. His name El-Shaddai (God Almighty) implies that He is more able and ready to pour out His grace than we are to receive it.

When we embrace the thought of His lavish and excessive grace toward us, we can do nothing more than humbly live in obedience to Him. God told Abram to walk before Him faithfully and be blameless. This is an invitation to us as well. He is God Almighty, the All-Sufficient One. He generously pours His unending and overwhelming grace upon us, and we are gently compelled to walk faithfully with Him.

*Thank You, Father, for Your limitless love toward Your own!*

*He Is...*

# Able

*Is anything too hard for the LORD?*
GENESIS 18:14

No matter how hard I try, there are certain things in life I simply cannot do. But God doesn't have a list of things He cannot do. It is in His capacity to do all things. Nothing is impossible for Him. When we can't see solutions, He does. When we think there is no hope, He knows better. He is able to bring beauty from ashes, calm through a storm, peace in the midst of chaos, and even joy from despair.

If God is able to do all things, why doesn't He put an end to suffering in this world? Answers aren't easy,[5] but there's one thing we know: He is not only able—He is kind. He doesn't force His will upon us, but rather allows us to make choices. And some of those choices cause pain. Our sufferings allow us to see God's ability to work beyond the challenges. They also make us long for heaven, where He will make all things right.

# Wants to Keep Us from Sin

*Yes, I know you did this with a clear conscience,*
*and so I have kept you from sinning against me.*

GENESIS 20:6

Abimelech took Sarah from Abraham in order to marry her. He thought she was Abraham's sister and didn't realize she was his wife. But God warned him in a dream because He knew that Abimelech had a clear conscience. He didn't want him to make this innocent mistake, so He gave him an opportunity (a choice) to turn from his sin.

God doesn't want us to sin. He knows that sin is destructive. It destroys our hearts, our lives, and our peace. We are beloved children, to whom He has granted the freedom to make choices. The Bible reminds us, "God is faithful; he will not let you be tempted beyond what you can bear. But when you are tempted, he will also provide a way out so that you can endure it."[6] As you face temptations throughout your day, look for the escape route that God has provided and ask for His help.

*He...*

# Opens Our Eyes

*God opened her eyes and she saw a well of water.*
GENESIS 21:19

There are times when our sight can be blinded by hopelessness or fear. Often we can become consumed with our circumstances and can't envision a solution. Hagar could not see any possibilities for her and her son. She thought they would simply die in the desert. Yet God not only heard her prayers, but He opened her eyes to His provision for her. He removed whatever was blinding her and keeping her from seeing the water she so desperately needed.

Interestingly, it doesn't say that He made the well of water for her; rather, it says He "opened her eyes." The well of water may have been there all along, but she couldn't see it. Do not assume that because you cannot see any hope or possibilities, none exist. Instead, ask God to open your eyes to the provisions around you. Ask Him to give you fresh eyes to see your situation from a new and a broader viewpoint.

# Sacrifice-Provider

*God himself will provide the lamb*
*for the burnt offering, my son.*
GENESIS 22:8

It was a tense moment. Isaac and Abraham were headed up the mountain to present a burnt offering to God, but there was no lamb. God was testing Abraham's heart to see if he would be willing to offer even his only son. Abraham prophetically stated a truth that would be fulfilled several thousand years later in Christ, when God provided the Lamb who died on our behalf.

The angel of the Lord stopped Abraham from offering Isaac. The Bible then tells us that Abraham looked up, and there in a thicket he saw a ram caught by its horns. He went over and took the ram and sacrificed it as a burnt offering instead of his son. So Abraham called that place "the LORD Will Provide." God provided a lamb that day on the mountain, and He has provided a lamb for all who will believe—Jesus, the Lamb of God who takes away the sins of the world.

*He Is...*

# Shiloh

*The scepter shall not depart from*
*Judah...until Shiloh comes.*

GENESIS 49:10 NKJV

The phrase "until Shiloh comes" can be translated, "Until he comes to whom the scepter belongs." The literal translation for the word *shiloh* is "sent." Jesus is the One who was sent from God. Certainly the scepter belongs to Him, for He is the Prince of Peace, God's only Son. It's interesting to note that Shiloh was also the name of the town that was the first permanent location of the tabernacle, thus making it the central location for worship. In Jeremiah the city of Shiloh is mentioned: "Go now to the place in Shiloh where I first made a dwelling for my Name."[7]

What does Shiloh mean to us personally? Jesus is our ruler, the one who holds the scepter in our lives. Just as the city of Shiloh was the dwelling place for God's name, so God's name rested on Jesus. He is our Shiloh, our central place to come to God. Through Him we are able to approach God's throne of grace.

*Thank You, Father, for sending Jesus, our Shiloh.*

*He Has...*

# Good Intentions

*You intended to harm me, but God intended
it for good to accomplish what is now
being done, the saving of many lives.*

**GENESIS 50:20**

God has a good purpose and a plan when everything seems impossible. Joseph was sold into slavery by his brothers, falsely accused by his employer, and forgotten in prison by his friends, yet God had a plan. When Joseph became second to Pharaoh and his brothers came to ask for mercy from him, he humbly recognized the hand of God. His desire was not to get back at his brothers, but to point to God's good plan.

When we go through a difficulty or a trial, especially one due to the fault of someone else, we must recognize that God can take even people's harmful actions and use them for good. Isaiah the prophet said about Christ, "It was the Lord's good plan to crush him." Yes, Jesus gives us the perfect picture of the good intentions of God.

# **The Great I Am**

*God said to Moses, "I AM WHO I AM."*
EXODUS 3:14

God is the only one who can claim, "I Am who I Am." This mighty declaration points to His own self-existence. He has always been, He is, and He will be forever. No one created Him, for He has always existed. As A.W. Tozer put it, "He is the Great Original."[8] The fact that He has always existed distinguishes Him as God and reminds us that we are not. He has no origin. We, the created, have a beginning. It is impossible for our finite minds to comprehend the infinite thought of the great I Am, and grasp the fact that He has always been and always will be.

The Self-Existent One who depends on no one invites us to depend on Him. How wonderful to know the great I Am as our loving Father and faithful Deliverer. He is the unchangeable God. He holds the wisdom of the ages, and yet is very real and present in our lives today.

*He Is Our…*

# Redeemer

*I will redeem you with an outstretched arm.*
Exodus 6:6

G od redeemed the Israelites through His outstretched arm and mighty acts. He is a redeeming God. He is able to bring freedom from slavery and hope through trials. Job went through great suffering, yet he also saw God's redemption. Through his pain he was able to say, "I know my Redeemer lives."

The ultimate redemption is the price that Christ paid to redeem us and purchase our salvation. Paul told believers, "In him we have redemption through his blood, the forgiveness of sins, in accordance with the riches of God's grace."[9] Rejoice in God our Redeemer! He redeemed the Israelites from slavery, Job from trials, and us from sin. Always remember that His redemptive power continues to work in powerful ways in our daily challenges and trials. He brings beauty from ashes. He is our Redeemer.

*He Is Our...*

# **Strong Defender**

*The LORD is my strength and my defense.*
EXODUS 15:2

We can feel alone, inadequate, or afraid when we face difficulties in our lives, yet there is a Strong One on whom we can depend. He is able to defend us, deliver us, and lead us onward. God rescued the Israelites from the hand of the Egyptians in a dramatic way. Once they crossed the Red Sea, Moses and the people of Israel sang a song of deliverance: "The LORD is my strength and my defense." The Israelites were helpless on their own, and they knew that their deliverance came from the mighty hand of God.

Sometimes we don't recognize God's strength until we understand our own weakness. It is easy for us to try to live and move in our own strength. It takes humility to lean on Him for strength and recognize that we can't do it all on our own. He is our strong one, our defender.

# **Right Hand Is Majestic**

*Your right hand, LORD,*
*was majestic in power.*
EXODUS 15:6

The right hand of the Lord is mentioned throughout Scripture. The psalmist declared, "Your right hand is filled with righteousness."[10] "Your hand is strong, your right hand exalted."[11] "Not by their sword that they won the land, nor did their arm bring them victory; it was your right hand, your arm, and the light of your face, for you loved them."[12] Victory came from God's right hand, not human hands.

What is the significance of the right hand? In patriarchal blessings, the right hand was the preferential one. Solemn oaths were made with an uplifted right hand. Christ is seated at the right hand of God, a place of honor and power. Our hands may be weak and feeble, but God's hands are majestic, righteous, strong, and able to deliver us. Isaiah said, "I am the LORD your God who takes hold of your right hand and says to you, 'Do not fear; I will help you.'"[13] How beautiful! Our right hand is in His.

# Makes Bitter Waters Sweet

*Moses threw it [the piece of wood] into the
water and the water turned sweet.*

Exodus 15:25 msg

As Moses led the Israelites from the Red Sea, they traveled for three days without finding water. When they finally found water it was bitter, yet instead of asking for God's help, the Israelites chose to grumble. Moses cried out to God, and God led him to a piece of wood, and when he threw it into the water, the waters were made sweet. God transformed bitter waters into sweet, and He is able to make something sweet out of our bitter circumstances as well.

The people grumbled, but Moses cried out to God. Who do you go to for your comfort? Look to God for your provision, and trust Him for His comfort and strength. Do not grumble. Instead remember that just as He used wood to turn the water into sweet refreshment, so He used the wooden cross to transform our lives and satisfy our thirsty souls.

# Banner

*Moses built an altar and called it The LORD is my Banner.*
EXODUS 17:15

The Israelites fought in an intense battle against the Amalekites. As long as Moses held his hands up, the Israelites were winning, but whenever he lowered his hands, the Amalekites dominated. What a funny way to do battle! Moses knew it wasn't his arms that did the work; it was the hand of God. At the end of the victorious battle Moses built an altar and declared, "The LORD is my Banner."

*Jehovah Nissi* (Hebrew for The LORD is my Banner) is descriptive of God's covering, His protection, His ownership, His power, His intervention. God is our banner, the One in whom we find victory. He fights for His people. Perhaps you are facing a battle in your life right now. Turn to Jehovah Nissi as your banner. He watches over you, providing power and protection.

*He Is a...*

# Jealous God

*I, the LORD your God, am a jealous God.*
EXODUS 20:5

It's easy to think of jealousy in terms of hatred and vengeance, because that's how people react when they are jealous. But we should not equate man's response to God's character, for they are very different. God alone is worthy of our worship, honor, and praise. The word "jealous" (*qanna* in Hebrew) refers directly to the attributes of His justice and holiness. Because He is holy He cannot tolerate sin, and because He is just, He cannot tolerate the worship of other gods.

Spurgeon spoke of God's jealousy in this way, "Since he is the only God, the Creator of heaven and earth, he cannot endure that any creature of his own hands, or fiction of a creature's imagination should be thrust into his throne, and be made to wear his crown."[14] God alone has the right to be jealous. His deep love for us, His beloved people, can only lead to wanting what is pure and best for us. He is jealous because He loves us.

# Sanctifies

*I am the LORD who sanctifies you.*
EXODUS 31:13 NKJV

God wanted His people to know throughout all generations that He is the Lord who sanctifies them. To sanctify means "to make holy." He makes us holy, because we cannot make ourselves holy. It is tempting to believe we can sanctify ourselves through our own good deeds and selfless acts. Our righteous acts are well and good and should come from an outpouring of our love for the Lord, but we must recognize that our righteous acts do not sanctify us or make us holy. Only He can sanctify us.

Many religions in our world today promote a type of self-sanctification or point system to earn heaven and holiness, but God's system is different. He sanctifies. He makes us holy through the blood of Christ. The purpose of Christ's giving His life for us on the cross was to give us His righteousness. It is not our righteousness, but His! We try to go back to sanctifying ourselves because grace is sometimes hard to comprehend and accept. Let us always remember that through faith in Christ we are sanctified.

*He Is...*

# Holy

*Be holy because I, the LORD your God, am holy.*
LEVITICUS 19:2

When Isaiah saw a glimpse of the Lord's glory and heard the angels declare, "Holy, holy, holy is the LORD Almighty," he could do nothing else but cry, "Woe to me, I am ruined! For I am a man of unclean lips."[15] When we consider the holiness of God, all we can do is fall to our knees recognizing our own depravity and sin. It is difficult to paint even a small picture of His holiness in our minds because we see no comparison here on earth. Tozer said that God's holiness "stands apart, unique, unapproachable, incomprehensible and unattainable."[16]

How can we His people possibly be holy? Only through the blood of Christ. Through Him we are purified and set apart as His special people. What a glorious and kind God we serve, who would allow us to be holy in His sight, without blemish and free from accusation![17] Take joy in the fact that we are made holy by His grace. The Holy One has made us holy.

*He Is a...*

# God of Order

*The Israelites are to camp around the Tent of Meeting...each of them under their standard and holding the banners of their family.*

NUMBERS 2:2

Order was essential as Moses led the Israelites through the wilderness. God established order through the structure of tribes and families. Throughout the Bible we see examples of God bringing order from chaos. We see it in creation, we see it in the wilderness, and we see it at the cross. We also see His ability to bring order into our own lives personally. Life is not orderly, but God is. Your life may seem chaotic, but He can bring order and peace to your heart.

Just as a referee brings order to a game, so the peace of Christ can bring order to our inner world. Paul wrote, "Let the peace of Christ rule in your hearts."[18] The word "rule" is actually a word meaning "umpire or referee." When you feel like life is a mess and everything is out of control, go to the God of order. Seek His help and let the peace of Christ bring order to your heart.

*He Has...*

# Powerful Arms

*The LORD answered Moses,
"Is the LORD's arm too short?"*

NUMBERS 11:23

God's people complained again and again during their wilderness experience. God told Moses that He would provide meat for the Israelites, but even Moses couldn't imagine how God would do it. That's when He answered, "Is the LORD's arm too short?" In other words, had the Lord's ability and power become inadequate or been thwarted somehow? Indeed it had not. God provided enough quail for the Israelites to eat to their heart's content. His arms are always able to reach out and provide in ways beyond what we can ask or imagine.

Is there an area of your life causing you to complain and grumble? Ask yourself, "Is the Lord's arm too short to help me? Has His ability been thwarted?" Often our complaining and grumbling reflect our lack of trust in God's provision. Turn your cares over to Him, trusting His loving and powerful arms to reach out and care for your needs.

*He Is...*

# Elohim

*God is not human, that he should lie,*
*not a human being, that he should change his mind.*

NUMBERS 23:19

God is not like a human being who may change his mind or go back on his word. Our God is God. He is reliable and trustworthy. He is able to keep every promise He utters, and He has the power to fulfill everything He declares. We can trust Him without suspicion. We can lean our whole weight into the God who is God.

The Hebrew name for God was *Elohim*, meaning omnipotent power. It refers to God's absolute dominion over all things in the entire universe. *El* means mighty or strong. We see it in words like El Shaddai (God Almighty) or El Elyon (God Most High). The interesting thing about the word "Elohim" is that the ending of the word (him) is plural. This does not imply that there is more than one God, but rather that God is one in three persons, Father, Son, and Spirit. In Deuteronomy we read, "The LORD [Jehovah] our God [Elohim], the LORD is one." [19] He is like no man; He is the one true God.

*He Is...*

# Faithful and True

*He is the faithful God, keeping his covenant*
*of love to a thousand generations.*

DEUTERONOMY 7:9

Faithful, and loyal; our Lord God keeps His promises to His people throughout the generations. He can be trusted. Perhaps you have felt the pain of a disloyal friend, an unfaithful spouse, or an unkind coworker. The pain can run deep when you have been betrayed. Our hearts long for someone we can believe in, someone we can trust, and someone who will always be faithful. The Lord your God is that faithful One. We can place our lives into His hands, for He will never abandon us or leave us. His faithfulness is sure.

He keeps His promises. He does not promise a perfect life or that our pathway will be challenge-free, but He does promise to be with us and be our strength through those rough times. He will never leave us or forsake us, His beloved followers. Take a moment right now to thank Him for His great faithfulness. Dwell on His faithful love throughout the day today.

# Defender of the Downtrodden

*He defends the cause of the fatherless and the widow.*
DEUTERONOMY 10:18

Compassion originated in the heart of the Creator. Our Father defends and cares for those who face difficulty, loss, and poverty. He is near to the brokenhearted and saves those who are crushed in spirit. Kindness is His nature and a fruit of His Spirit. Throughout the Bible we see that God has always shown care for the less fortunate. As His beloved people we reflect His love as we reach out and help those with needs both physically and spiritually.

God demonstrated the ultimate mercy and kindness by sending Jesus to rescue us from our spiritual poverty. As recipients of His grace, let us show grace toward our neighbors. We are His hands and feet to strengthen the weary and assist those who are oppressed. Ask God to open your eyes to the needs around you and show you how to reach out and help those in need.

# Works Are Perfect

*He is the Rock, his works are perfect.*
DEUTERONOMY 32:4

Michelangelo is considered by many to be the greatest artist of all times. The words "flawless" and "superhuman" have been used to describe some of his works. Michelangelo's work may be close to perfection, but God's work *is* perfect. He knows exactly what He is doing with every stroke of His creative hand, and His works are righteous because He is upright and just. He makes no mistakes.

It is easy to question God's ways or why He has allowed certain things to happen in our lives. Although His ways are perfect, people are not. We cannot completely understand His sovereignty and how it interacts with the will of man, but we can trust what we know about God. We know that His works are flawless. What may seem like a mistake from our perspective may fit into a beautiful divine tapestry that perfectly expresses an eternal picture.

*Father, we praise You, for Your ways are perfect. We trust Your work because You are upright and just.*

*He...*

# Takes Vengeance

*It is mine to avenge; I will repay.*
DEUTERONOMY 32:35

Revenge! It's always been a common theme of big-screen action movies, and even more so today. God says *He* will avenge. He will repay the enemy. In the book of Romans we see this phrase repeated with clear instructions for us as believers:

> Do not take revenge, my dear friends, but leave room for God's wrath, for it is written: "It is mine to avenge; I will repay," says the Lord... "If your enemy is hungry, feed him; if he is thirsty, give him something to drink. In doing this, you will heap burning coals on his head." Do not be overcome by evil, but overcome evil with good. [20]

Are you willing to leave vengeance in the Lord's hands? Certainly we must set wise boundaries so we do not allow someone to hurt or abuse us, and we recognize the importance of civil punishment. Yet we must recognize God as the ultimate avenger. Instead of getting back at someone, overcome evil with good, and leave the vengeance to God.

# Drives Out Our Enemies

*He drives out the enemy before you.*
DEUTERONOMY 33:27 NLT

Close your eyes right now and picture His everlasting arms under you, carrying you and protecting you from your enemies. Our passage today begins with this reassurance: "There is no one like the God of Israel. He rides across the heavens to help you, across the skies in majestic splendor. The eternal God is your refuge, and His everlasting arms are under you. *He drives out the enemy before you.*" Isn't that wonderful?

This passage doesn't guarantee that our lives will be free from enemies. Even Jesus had enemies. But it does guarantee that as God's precious children, He is our refuge. We are held in His everlasting arms. He who can destroy our enemies with a word will allow only what is necessary to pass through His loving embrace. Just as protective parents will go to great lengths for the welfare of their children, so the Lord rides across the heavens to help you and hold you.

*He Is a...*

# Giving God

*Take possession of the land the LORD our God
is giving you for your own.*

JOSHUA 1:11

God loves to give. He gave the Promised Land to His people, but even more important, He gave His only Son on our behalf. God not only gives, but He gives sacrificially. He gives willingly. He gives mercifully. He gives good and perfect gifts. Because He loves us He also gives us discipline for our growth, so that we may become mature and complete, not lacking anything. If a human father knows how to give good gifts to his children, how much more will our Father in heaven give good gifts to those who ask Him![21]

How does God's nature of giving impact you and me? Because He has given us so much, we in turn ought to reflect His giving nature by giving to others. What can we give? Our time, our hearts, our help, our material possessions, our encouragement, our patience, our gifts, our talents, our hope, and our forgiveness. Consider the ways God wants you to reflect His beautiful attribute of giving.

*He Is...*

# Amazing!

*Tomorrow the LORD will do amazing things among you.*
JOSHUA 3:5

Although the word *amazing* may be overused, we should never become tired of the amazing things God has done. As the Israelites got ready to enter the Promised Land, Joshua attempted to prepare them for God's amazing plan. As the priests carrying the ark of the Lord set foot in the Jordan, the water upstream stopped flowing and the Israelites were able to walk on dry ground. God brought down the walls of Jericho and gloriously led His people into the Promised Land.

Let us never lose our sense of awe as we observe His amazing deeds. We can look with wonder at the beauty of the night sky and the magnificent display of stars and see His amazing handiwork. We can relish the preciousness of a newborn child and be awed by the intricate way God forms each one of us. May we always rejoice as we watch God work in amazing and simple ways in our daily lives.

# Peace

*Gideon built an altar to the LORD there
and called it The LORD Is Peace.*

JUDGES 6:24

The world is filled with all different sorts of battles. There are always countries at war, but what about the wars happening right around you? In our culture today we see husbands and wives battling with one another. We see embattled churches and even friends and neighbors in disagreement. Perhaps the most common war of all is the war within our own hearts and minds with anxiety or unrest. No matter what kind of war surrounds us, we can go to the God of peace (*Jehovah Shalom*) and seek His comfort.

Ask the God of peace to give you His peace in the midst of your battle. Cast all your worries and cares on Him, for the Bible reassures us that the "peace of God that transcends all understanding will guard our hearts and minds in Christ Jesus."[22] God's peace begins in our own hearts and then overflows into the relationships and situations around us.

# Becomes Angry

*Because the Israelites forsook the LORD and no
longer served him, he became angry with them.*

JUDGES 10:7

As much as we would like to focus only on God's love
and mercy, we must also recognize that He
becomes angry. What stirred up God's anger? The Bible
tells us that His beloved people did evil in His eyes and
served other gods. Instead of turning steadfastly toward
Him, they chose to forsake Him again and again. They
tested His patience.

God is generous in His patience toward His people,
and He will not harbor His anger forever. Throughout the Old Testament we see the gracious love God
extended toward the Israelites. David wrote, "His anger
lasts only a moment, but his favor lasts a lifetime."[23] He
is slow to anger and abounding in love. His kindness
draws us to repentance and obedience. Let us not test
His patience, but rather turn to Him and adore Him.

*He Is Our...*

# **Provider**

*Praise the LORD, who has now
provided a redeemer for your family!*
RUTH 4:14 NLT

Naomi must have felt as though life was over. Her husband and two sons had died, and now she was left with her daughters-in-law in a foreign country. But God had a plan and a provision that went far beyond what she could imagine. As Naomi returned to her homeland, her daughter-in-law Ruth stayed with her. Eventually Ruth married Boaz, Naomi's kinsman, who redeemed her. The child born to Ruth and Boaz grew to be the grandfather of King David!

The story of Ruth offers us a picture of God's good plan. We may not understand why difficulties and sorrows come our way, or why our life hasn't turned out as we thought it would. It is in these times we must trust God as our provider, recognizing that His ways are perfect and He has a plan bigger than what we can see. He provides redemption in wonderful and unexpected ways.

*He Is the...*

# Rock

*There is no Rock like our God.*

1 SAMUEL 2:2

S olid, strong, immovable, unshakable, impenetrable—
these are a few words that come to mind when I
think about a giant rock formation. But God is far more
than these simple human descriptions, for there is no
Rock like Him. We can stand firm on His unchanging
strength, and we can depend upon Him as a sure and
immovable foundation. Just as a house that is built on
a rock foundation doesn't falter, so our lives built upon
Him as our Rock stand firm.

It's so easy to look at other objects that seem like
rocks (people, money, things, and so on), assuming
they will provide strength and security for our lives. Yet
our passage today reminds us there is no one else like
the Lord, no other Rock like Him. Where do you find
your strength and your sure footing in life? On whom
do you depend? Look to the Lord your Rock and find
your firm foundation.

*He Has...*

# Different Vision

*People look at the outward appearance,*
*but the LORD looks at the heart.*

1 SAMUEL 16:7

God doesn't look at people the way we look at people. We tend to make an appraisal of others based on what we see outwardly. But thankfully, God is different. He looks at the heart. He can see people's motives, intentions, character, and faith. To Him, it's not about what we look like on the outside—rather, He is concerned about what is found deep within us.

We tend to make assumptions about a person's character or their motives, but we must humbly recognize that God alone knows the intent of the heart. Jesus told the Pharisees that what is in a person's heart comes out through their mouths. Let us listen to the words of others and hear their hearts instead of rushing into judgment. Most important, let's ask God to create in us a clean heart.

*He Is the...*

# Lord of Heaven's Armies

*I come to you in the name of the*
*Lord of Heaven's Armies.*

1 Samuel 17:45 nlt

As David confronted Goliath, his confidence wasn't in himself but in the Lord of Heaven's Armies, God Almighty. Legions of angels stand ready at His word. Jesus said on the night He was betrayed, "Do you think I cannot call on my Father, and he will at once put at my disposal more than twelve legions of angels?"[24]

How grand the magnitude of heaven's armies! In Chronicles we find King Hezekiah reassuring His people, "Be strong and courageous. Do not be afraid or discouraged because of the king of Assyria and the vast army with him, for there is a greater power with us than with him. With him is only the arm of flesh, but with us is the Lord our God to help us and to fight our battles."[25] No matter what battle you are facing, look to the Lord of Heaven's Armies for your strength.

*He...*

# Guides

*In the course of time, David inquired of the LORD.*
2 SAMUEL 2:1

When it came to directions, David didn't hesitate to ask. More importantly he brought his inquiry to the right source, the Lord God who knows all and sees all. In humility David inquired of Him for guidance. David asked whether he should move back to Judah, and even asked which town he should go to. The Lord answered him and directed him. Psalm 23 says, "He guides me along the right path bringing honor to His name."

As we seek God for direction, He is faithful to lead us down the right path, bringing honor to His name. He may lead us with a still, small voice, or through a change in circumstance, or through the wise counsel of others. When you face decisions or forks in the road, remember He is your guide. Inquire of Him. Seek His guidance and listen as He leads the way.

*He...*

# Whispers

*After the fire there was the sound of a gentle whisper.*
1 KINGS 19:12

When you want to get someone's attention, try a gentle whisper. It can be much more effective than a loud harsh voice. God chose to speak to Elijah, not in the strong wind, nor in an earthquake or even a fire, but rather in a gentle whisper. Isn't He surprising? In a whisper He drew Elijah's attention and stilled his spirit. God may choose to speak in dramatic ways, but often He speaks in ways that require us to be attentive and listen for His voice.

Aren't you glad God is gentle? His gentle voice of conviction doesn't riddle us with ear-piercing bullets of guilt, but rather kindly and tenderly points us back to Him. He gently guides us through the wisdom of His Word, the Bible. He whispers, "I love you, My precious child." We must be still in order to hear His voice.

*He Is to Be...*

# Feared Above All

*He is to be feared above all gods.*
1 Chronicles 16:25

God is loving, compassionate, and gracious, yet He is also to be feared. We must live with a healthy reverence for His holiness, righteousness, and justice. To fear Him is to honor Him, recognizing His greatness and His ability to do all things. To fear Him means to humbly recognize that all I have comes from Him and without Him I could do nothing. The Lord is to be feared because He is the mighty Creator and Lord over all. He is slow to anger, but He also brings judgment.

Fearing Him means we recognize that He is in charge of this world, and we are not. He is sovereign, yet we have limited understanding. He sees all, while we see only a snapshot of life and eternity. Just as we would be filled with awe if we were granted an audience with a king, so we must live in humble awe as we have the joy of living in our King's presence every day.

# Owns the Battle

*The battle is not yours, but God's.*
2 CHRONICLES 20:15

King Jehoshaphat was up against what seemed like insurmountable odds. A vast and mighty army had come against Him, and it seemed as if defeat was inevitable. But with God there is always hope. Jehoshaphat humbly came before the Lord and sought His help. He placed all his trust in the Lord, saying, "We do not know what to do, but our eyes are upon you."

Jehoshaphat didn't know what to do, but he certainly knew who to go to. He turned His eyes off of his enemy and placed them on the Lord. He focused on God's strength and kindness. God so wonderfully reassured Jehoshaphat that He would fight the battle for him, and He did! When God fights our battles, He gets the glory. Let us turn our eyes toward Him as we face the battles of life, whether large or small. He brings victory in unexpected ways. He is glorified in our lives as we give Him our battles.

# Compassionate

*The LORD your God is gracious and compassionate.*
*He will not turn his face from you if you return to him.*
2 CHRONICLES 30:9

Our God not only sees our pain, but He is compassionate toward our condition. *Compassion* is a beautiful word. The root word *passion* actually means "suffering." Compassion basically means "together with suffering." God is gracious toward those who turn to Him, and He joins together with them in their pain. God created us, He knows us, and He sees our need for forgiveness, help, and mercy.

The passion of the cross, Christ's suffering for us, was the ultimate gift of compassion. Our sin separated us from God, but God compassionately provided a way for us to be forgiven. Just as the Israelites were invited to return to the Lord, so we are invited to place our faith in Christ. He will not turn His face from you if you turn to Him. He is compassionate and gracious, slow to anger and abounding in love.

# Determined Earth's Dimensions

*Who marked off its dimensions? Surely you know!*
*Who stretched a measuring line across it?*

JOB 38:5

Job didn't understand why a myriad of terrible trage-dies happened to him. In His wisdom, God chose not to give Job a direct answer, but rather to ask him a series of questions. He began with, "Where were you when I laid the earth's foundation? Tell me, if you understand." He went on to point out every aspect of creation to demonstrate that His ways are far beyond comprehension.

God designed the dimensions of the earth to a perfect degree of accuracy. Scientists recognize that our planet is the "perfect size" to sustain life. Among many other things, if the earth were smaller, the gravitational pull would be affected and life-giving oxygen would leave our atmosphere. If it were any bigger, additional poisonous chemicals would be held in our atmosphere. God marked off the exact dimensions as He created our world. Let us trust the Designer of the universe with the design of our lives.

# Sends Rain to the Desert

*Who cuts a channel for the torrents of rain ... to water*
*a land where no one lives, an uninhabited desert?*

Job 38:25-26

When land is dry and parched, it is God who brings water once again. He can provide refreshing rain to uninhabited deserts. There are times in each of our lives when we feel as though we are in a desert. Let us remember that if God brings water to land where no one lives, then He can bring hope to our desolation as well. Although a place may be uninhabited, it is not outside of His watch-care. There is no situation so far away that He will not bring help. There is no circumstance that is dried up to the point that He gives up.

God brings refreshment and renewal to the unexpected and parched places. Pour out your heart to the One who sees even when no one else seems to see. Cry out to the One who brings healing water to your desert. He loves you and is able to meet your needs right where you are.

# Cannot Be Corrected

*Will the one who contends with*
*the Almighty correct Him?*
JOB 40:2

How many times have you had to say, "I was wrong"? I've had to do that more times than I'd like to admit. We are human, we make mistakes, and we need to be corrected at times. But not God! We may not understand why He allows things to happen, but we do know He doesn't make mistakes. A teacher may correct a student's paper, and a parent may correct a child's behavior, but no one can correct the Lord.

Some people shake their fist at God in anger, not agreeing with what He has done. Others, like Job, wonder why God has allowed a good man to go through difficulties. Sometimes we may question His ways or even attempt to tell Him how we would have done things differently, yet He does not need further instructions. Although it may be difficult, we must trust Him as the Sovereign Creator and Lord over all.

*Thank You, Father, that our lives are in Your hands, the hands of a God who makes no mistakes.*

# Cannot Be Thwarted

*I know that you can do all things;*
*no purpose of yours can be thwarted.*

JOB 42:2

When was the last time your plans were thwarted? On any given day our plans may be redirected, realigned, and reworked. But not God's plans. No purpose of His can be thwarted. He is un-thwartable! We cannot mess up His purposes. Job declared this truth about God after he had been through some of life's worst tragedies. He lost his possessions, his children, and his health. Surely there was some mistake—surely God's purposes for Job got mixed up with someone else's blueprints, right?

Not according to Job. As he wrestled with understanding why this happened, God made it clear that His plans and purposes are much bigger than what we can see. He is in control of the entire universe. Nothing slips through His fingers. Nothing messes up His plans. His ways are not our ways. No one can disrupt the purpose He has set out for us.

*He Is a...*

# Shield

*You, O Lord, are a shield for me,*
*my glory and the One who lifts up my head.*

Psalm 3:3 NKJV

David wrote this psalm when he fled from his own son Absalom as he attempted to take over the kingdom.[26] It was possibly one of the lowest moments in his life. His very own son was intentionally humiliating him. David had no guarantee how this terrible situation would turn out, yet his eyes were on the Lord. He knew that God was his protector, shield, and lifter of his head. He knew that whatever happened, God would guard his reputation.

No matter what challenges you are facing, no matter what humiliation or hurt you are going through from another person or even a family member, you can look to the Lord as your shield. He is your defender and your protector. He may allow difficulties into your life. Do not be discouraged or defeated, for He is your shield to protect you in the battle. Look to Him and trust Him to guard your heart and your reputation.

*He Is...*

# Just

*I will thank the LORD because he is just.*
**PSALM 7:17 NLT**

When we see someone wronged, or when we have been wronged ourselves, we want justice. The psalmist likens God's justice to the great deep. On the surface of the ocean all we see is waves and white foam, but underneath is a different story. Beneath the ocean's surface there is a whole different world; a place populated by sea life and teeming with activity. In the same way, we may not see the movement of God's justice from our point of view, but He is working in ways we cannot begin to fathom.

The apostle Paul wrote, "Oh, the depth of the riches of the wisdom and knowledge of God! How unsearchable his judgments, and his paths beyond tracing out!"[27] Knowing the depth of God's justice frees us from vengeance. Paul later added, "Do not take revenge, my dear friends, but leave room for God's wrath, for it is written: 'It is mine to avenge; I will repay,' says the Lord."[28]

*Thank You, Father, for Your justice in Your time in Your way.*

*He Is the...*

# Majestic Lord

*LORD, our Lord,*
*how majestic is your name in all the earth!*

Psalm 8:1

The title *Lord* is the Hebrew word *Adonai*. It means "The Lord, my great Lord." He is the Master and the Majestic One. The term *Lord* actually implies ownership and serves as a reminder that God is our total authority and master of all. Yet He is not a cruel or unjust taskmaster. As our loving Lord, He guides us down the right path and equips us for the tasks He calls us to do. We can safely put our trust in our kind and good master. We bring honor to Him through both our obedience and our trust.

The question is, do you serve Him as Lord of your life, or do you view Him simply as a god of convenience, here to serve you and answer your prayers? Let us recommit ourselves to our great Lord and Master, willingly seeking and serving Him with our whole hearts.

*His...*

# Laws Are Perfect

*The law of the LORD is perfect,*
*refreshing the soul.*

PSALM 19:7

When we think of laws it's easy to picture rules that weigh us down or keep us from doing something. God's laws don't detract from life; they give life. God's laws are perfect, restoring and reviving us. Just as eating healthy food strengthens our bodies, so following God's laws nourishes and enriches our souls. What is the law of the Lord? It is His instructions and commands. His Word is the place we go for His teaching and to learn His will for man, so that we may walk in obedience.

The psalmist prayed, "Open my eyes that I may see wonderful things in your law."[29] God gives us laws to protect us and make us wise. Let us look at His laws with love and adoration and not despise them. They are a wonderful and perfect gift that restores and strengthens us in the very core of our being.

*Father, thank You for Your perfect law. It strengthens me as a person.*

*His...*

# Precepts Are Right

*The precepts of the LORD are right,*
*giving joy to the heart.*

PSALM 19:8

God's precepts are right, and they bring joy to our heart. The word *precept* refers to basic life principles on which we can stand. God has lovingly given us precepts and guidelines as to how to live life and interact with others. When we follow them, we experience joy in life. On the other hand, when we choose to go the other way and ignore them, we face heartache and sadness. Only God knows what will bring joy to our lives.

Additionally, the psalmist wrote that God's commands are radiant. They shine brilliantly and brightly with perfection. They light up our path so we can see which direction to go in life. They bring light to our eyes, helping us understand things that unbelievers cannot see. Let us be devoted to getting to know God's precepts and commands by studying His Word and living them out in our daily lives.

# All We Need

*The Lord is my Shepherd;*
*I have all that I need.*
Psalm 23:1 nlt

Sheep are not able to take care of themselves; they are totally dependent on the shepherd for all of their needs. God is our Shepherd, and He takes care of our needs. He lovingly cares for us. Even when we don't know what we need, He is aware of all our needs both inward and outward. What we think we need, may not be best for us. He is the All-Sufficient One.

David, while tending his flocks, recognized that there was a greater Shepherd tending to his needs. There in the wilderness the young shepherd knew that God completely fulfilled the longings of his heart. God is all we need spiritually. He provides comfort for our soul. He strengthens our spirit, and most important, He supplies forgiveness of sin through Christ. As His precious sheep, dear to His very heart, let us look to Him as the one who meets our needs, spiritually, emotionally, and physically.

*Father, our eyes are on You. In You we have all that we need.*

# Leads Us Beside Peaceful Streams

*He leads me beside peaceful streams.*
PSALM 23:2 NLT

Sheep have only a few basic needs. They need green meadows for eating and resting, and they need peaceful streams from which to drink. Sheep will not drink from raging waters or streams that are flowing too fast. They will drink only from streams with a gentle flow. A good shepherd knows exactly what they need, and he leads them to the perfect place. Do you trust the Shepherd to lead you to a place to truly quench your thirst? As His sheep, we may think we know which way we should go to find the best way to quench our thirst and nourish our souls, yet our Shepherd knows best.

I'm thankful that God doesn't lead us to busy, frenetic, and overwhelming meadows to feed us. He leads us to a place where we can feed and rest. Jesus said, "Come unto me, all who are weary, and I will give you rest." Jesus brought comfort and rest.

*Wonderful Shepherd, thank You for bringing rest to my weary soul.*

# Renews Our Strength

*He renews my strength.*
*He guides me down the right paths,*
*Bringing honor to His name.*
PSALM 23:3 NLT

Have you ever felt like you didn't have the strength to go on? Perhaps you were worn out physically and didn't think you could make it to the finish line. Maybe you are mentally exhausted from studying or trying to get through a project. It could be emotional exhaustion, when you have faced challenge after challenge with family or work. Thankfully, we can go to our Shepherd, who renews our strength.

As we follow Him, He guides us down paths that can bring renewal and strength. At those times when we feel exhausted, we can ask the Shepherd for strength and guidance. If we continue to forge ahead in our own strength, who gets the glory? Yet when we look to Him for guidance and help, His name is honored.

*He Is...*

# Close Beside Us

*Even when I walk through the darkest valley,*
*I will not be afraid, for you are close beside me.*

Psalm 23:4 nlt

You are not alone. Your Shepherd is close beside you. He protects and comforts you in the midst of your darkest valleys. Do not be afraid, for you do not walk your path by yourself. It is a great comfort to know that when we face the scariest times in our lives, He is there with us. The Bible doesn't say that we will never walk through dark times, but it does reassure us that we won't walk through them alone.

What great assurance we have in knowing that the Lord our God will not leave us. Do not fear about things that may happen or the possibility of valleys in your life. The what-ifs need not linger as long as we remember that our good Shepherd will protect and comfort us in their midst. Let us walk in confidence and not fear for the road ahead.

# Prepares a Feast for Us

*You prepare a feast for me*
*in the presence of my enemies.*
PSALM 23:5

Imagine enjoying a great and glorious banquet while those who have tried to hurt you or have plotted evil against you watch with envy. David is giving an illustration of the Lord's kindness to His people as well as the triumph He brings over their enemies. As much as we would love to go through this life with no enemies, it is highly unlikely that we will. David was a man after God's own heart, yet he had enemies. Jesus even had many enemies. Although we may have enemies in this world, we can also be assured that God will bring redemption.

Do not be discouraged by those who seem to be against you. Instead, pray for your enemies and allow God to bring justice in His time. He will strengthen and feed you. The ultimate feast will be the banquet of all banquets, the marriage supper of the Lamb described in Revelation. He is preparing a place for His own to feast at His table.

*He Is the...*

# Light of Our Lives

*The LORD is my light and my salvation—*
*whom shall I fear?*

PSALM 27:1

Light is one of the most powerful deterrents to crime, and the light of the Lord is one of the most powerful deterrents to our fears. When the Lord is our light we do not live in the darkness of fear or worry, because we are in the hands of our sovereign and powerful Lord. Fear does not have much room to grow when we place our trust in God. David knew that God was his salvation and his stronghold, and he lived each day confidently in Him.

What fears or worries are you carrying around with you today? Will you place them in the hands of your loving Lord? Faith says, "I don't need to live in fear, for my God is my strength. He is my light and my salvation. He will guide me and comfort me. He will never leave me." Let us step forward in the light of His love today.

*He...*

# Carries Us

*Save your people and bless your inheritance;*
*be their shepherd and carry them forever.*

PSALM 28:9

In the last few months of his life, Hudson Taylor told a friend, "I am so weak I cannot write. I cannot read my Bible. I cannot even pray. All I can do is lie still in the arms of God as a little child, trusting Him."[30] There are times when we feel as though we cannot take another step forward. All we can do is be still and like a child rest in God's precious arms. It is in our most difficult hours that God carries us. His arms are able and strong and can hold us close when we feel like we can't go on.

In Isaiah we read about God's comfort for His people: "He tends his flock like a shepherd: He gathers the lambs in his arms and carries them close to his heart."[31] My friend, keep your eyes on Him. In times of difficulty, do not despair. Picture yourself being carried by your loving Father as He holds you close to His heart.

*He Has a...*

# Powerful Voice

*The voice of the LORD is powerful;*
*the voice of the LORD is majestic.*

PSALM 29:4

With His voice God spoke the universe into being and creation into order. David wrote, "The voice of the LORD breaks the cedars; the LORD breaks in pieces the cedars of Lebanon."[32] Now cedar trees can grow up to 120 feet high with a circumference of 30 feet. It takes a powerful voice to break a tree of that stature.

In the New Testament God's voice declared "This is my Beloved Son." God's voice is still speaking to us through His Word and through His gentle and quiet Spirit within us. His voice is great, but He will not force His voice on us. We are reminded in Revelation that He stands at the door and knocks. If anyone hears His voice and opens the door, He will come in and dine with him. Are you listening to His voice, or do the busyness of life and the cares of this world drown out the majestic and powerful voice of your loving Lord?

*His...*

# Face Shines

*Let your face shine on your servant;*
*save me in your unfailing love.*

PSALM 31:16

The Bible is clear that God is a spiritual being, so what does it mean when we read references to the face of God? In Chronicles, God's people are encouraged to humble themselves, pray, and seek God's face.[33] In Psalms we read that God's eyes and ears are attentive to the righteous, but His face is against those who do evil.[34] The face of God obviously refers to the attention God gives to His people.

When we want a child's attention we ask them to turn their face toward us. When we want God's attention we humbly pray for Him to turn His face toward us. Sadly, those who do evil do not desire His attention, and so He turns His face in another direction, away from them. Let us be among the ones who invite His attention to shine upon us, saying, "Restore us, O God; make your face shine on us, that we may be saved."[35]

*He...*

# Answers When We Call

*This poor man called, and the LORD heard him;*
*he saved him out of all his trouble.*

**PSALM 34:6**

In the world of digitally recorded phone messages it's easy to feel as though no one is listening. Our scripture today reminds us that God is listening; we can always go to Him. The psalmist went to God with his troubles, and God delivered him. It's good to know that we too can call on the Lord with our concerns or worries.

Often when we face fears, we call on everyone but the Lord. Sometimes He is the last resort. Let us be determined to seek Him first and bring our cares to Him. He will answer with a peace that passes understanding. When we call, God answers. He never puts us on hold or refuses to listen. He doesn't grow tired of us coming to Him. His response may not be the exact way we anticipated, but we can trust His kindness and goodness to do what is best. Call on Him. He loves to hear from you.

*He Is...*

# Good

*Taste and see that the LORD is good;*
*blessed is the one who takes refuge in him.*

PSALM 34:8

To describe something as "good" means that it is pleasant or delightful. In this psalm, David invites the reader to investigate or take a convincing bite of God's goodness. Just as a person who has sampled a delicious morsel of food says, "This is good. You should try some," so David has personally tasted of God's goodness and now he wants us to do the same.

David encourages us to step forward and trust the Lord, so that we too will perceive that God is desirable and delightful. Are you willing to take refuge in Him and experience the delightful flavor of God's goodness? Go ahead and try a taste of trusting Him with all your heart. Blessed and satisfied is the person who takes refuge in Him.

# Fountain of Life

*With you is the fountain of life;*
*in your light we see light.*

PSALM 36:9

God provides water from His river of delights, which is able to quench our thirsty souls. Our souls thirst for love and acceptance just as our bodies crave water. It's easy for all of us to try to find satisfaction and fulfillment in our status or work or people or things. Yet these always leave our soul longing for more. There is only One who can quench the deep thirst within us. His wellspring never runs dry. When we drink of Him we receive life—eternal life and abundant life.

A fountain offers a delightful picture of a refreshing flow of water. If you have ever been hot and thirsty on a summer day, you know the soothing comfort that you feel when you drink water from a cold fountain. Let us drink from the refreshing fountain of life that only God can offer. His water flows abundantly and freely.

*Father, we come to Your fountain to drink from Your river of delights.*

# Laughs at the Wicked

*The Lord laughs at the wicked,*
*for he knows their day is coming.*

PSALM 37:13

The wicked arrogantly scoff at God and His people, but He has the last laugh. He knows what is in store for them in the future. The plans of the wicked eventually fade away and their power will be broken, but the Bible tells us that God upholds the righteous. Their lives are in His hands.

At the beginning of this psalm, David reminds us, "Do not fret because of those who are evil or be envious of those who do wrong...Trust in the LORD and do good; dwell in the land and enjoy safe pasture." Let us get our eyes off the wicked and put our trust in the Lord. He sees, He knows, and He laughs at the arrogance of the wicked, for He is well aware that their day is coming.

*Father, thank You that You've got everything under control, and we can trust You and Your plan for the wicked.*

# Knows Our Secrets

*He knows the secrets of every heart.*
PSALM 44:21 NLT

The center of our emotions, the human heart, is complex and mysterious. Who among us is able to discern their own hidden faults or see the blind spots deep within their soul? We can't begin to know the secrets of our own hearts, but we know the One who does. God understands us, and thankfully He also has mercy on us. He penetrates deep within our heart. Nothing is a surprise to Him. Nothing is hidden from Him.

Our hearts are safe with Him. We can look to Him to comfort our deepest hurts and fulfill our emotional longings. He cleans our hearts from sin and gently reveals to us destructive habits. He gives strength to our hearts when we feel as though we cannot go on. Just as a skilled heart surgeon operates on the body's heart, so the Great Physician is able to mend the holes deep within our hearts. Will you trust your heart to His care? He who knows the secrets of every heart is able to help and heal yours.

# Here Among Us

*The LORD of Heaven's Armies is here among us.*
PSALM 46:7 NLT

What a marvelous comfort to know that the Lord of Heaven's Armies is here among us! Surely these words gave inspiration and hope to David and the armies of Israel as they faced their many battles. David knew the truth of these words from a personal standpoint, having faced Goliath and other powerful foes. He was able to stand in what would otherwise have been terrifying situations because he knew God was there with him.

We too can find help and hope in these words. The Lord of Heaven's Armies is here among us. Take a moment to dwell on that truth. Like the president visiting the troops, the Commander of the Lord's armies is in the camp. Close your eyes and say those words softly to yourself right now: "The Lord is here among us." Hold on to these words and let them strengthen you throughout your day.

# Causes Wars to End

*He causes wars to end throughout the earth.*
PSALM 46:9

Although wars may appear to us to be out of control, they are not out of God's control. He can cause them to end. So why doesn't He cause all wars to end? Why does He allow them to continue, when they bring such heartache, hatred, and death? There are no easy answers to that question, but I do know that He allows difficulties and tragedies for a greater purpose. He allows men and women to make choices, sometimes terrible ones, which still work into His sovereign plan.

The truth and comfort we can hold onto from this verse is that we know God's dominion is ultimately over all, and He knows the timing of every battle. Sometimes He may use the ugliness of war for certain purposes. Are you willing to trust Him even if you can't understand all His reasons and ways?

# King over All

*God is the King of all the earth;*
*sing to him a psalm of praise.*

PSALM 47:7

Most little girls dream of one day meeting a king like the ones we read about in fairy tales. As we grow, we leave behind the fairy tales, yet that youthful longing in our hearts to have an audience with royalty still lingers. It is amazing to think that the King of all the earth has chosen us to be His people and allowed us to be a part of His kingdom. It's humbling to realize we can approach His throne of grace boldly because of what Christ did for us on the cross.

The writer of Hebrews urges us as followers of Christ, "Let us then approach God's throne of grace with confidence, so that we may receive mercy and find grace to help us in our time of need."[36] As daughters of the High King of heaven, we can come before His throne knowing that we have been granted His favor. May we honor our King in what we say and do...and as the psalmist said, "Sing to him a song of praise."

*He Is Our...*

# Strength

*O my Strength, to you I sing praises,*
*for you, O God, are my refuge,*
*the God who shows me unfailing love.*

PSALM 59:17 NLT

When we are weak, He makes us strong. At times we may feel emotionally feeble, spiritually low, or physically frail, yet it is in those moments we can go to our Father and seek His rescue and His strength. He gives strength to the weary and increases the power of the weak.

He is the everlasting God, the Creator of the ends of the earth. He will never grow tired or weary. His strength is unlimited, and we can go to the well that never runs dry and receive strength from Him to carry on in our journey. Turn to Him and trust Him in your weak moments. Look to Him. Those who hope in the Lord will renew their strength. They will soar on wings like eagles as He becomes the wind—the strength— under their wings. [37]

# Place of Safety

*You have been my refuge,*
*a place of safety when I am in distress.*

PSALM 59:16

God is our safe place. Our hearts are safe with Him. We can pour them out to Him and cast our cares on Him, and not have to worry that He will condemn us or gossip about us. We can find refuge during the storms of life within His loving arms. Circumstances and people cannot always be trusted, but our God is a safe place and a trusted shelter when we are in distress.

David begins this psalm by saying, "I will sing of your love, for you have been my refuge." God's unfailing love for us is shown by the fact that He is our refuge and safe place. Not only does He have the power and ability to protect us, but in His loving-kindness He embraces us no matter where we are or how badly we have messed up. Run to Him as your place of safety in the hurricanes of life.

# Shakes and Mends

*You have shaken the land and torn it open;*
*mend its fractures, for it is quaking.*
PSALM 60:2

There are times when the Lord allows our world to be shaken. He has the power and authority to make the earth tremble. Because of His mercy and kindness we are not consumed, for He could cause our world to be torn completely apart at the mere sound of His voice. Whether God has allowed a literal earthquake or has allowed our personal lives to be shaken up, we know ultimately that we are in His hands. He not only shakes, He also mends.

He is the One who can mend our fractured lives. The same powerful hand that makes the earth tremble also brings calm to our storms and renewal to our lives. He is able to put back the shattered pieces of our brokenness. Although His hands are powerful and fearful, they are also loving and healing. Turn to Him for mending when your life seems to be falling apart. He is able to restore and make things new.

# Father to the Fatherless

*A father to the fatherless, a defender of widows,
is God in his holy dwelling.*

PSALM 68:5

When you think of a father in a family, what adjectives come to mind? Typically we think of someone who offers leadership, provision, protection, and direction. A good father is compassionate, kind, understanding, and helpful. To those who have felt abandoned by their earthly father, this verse from Psalms brings comfort and reassurance. God is a Father to those who have no one to call their father.

More important, He fills the hole in our heart, no matter what our family situation has been. Most people desire a good and pleasant relationship with their father. Some people spend their lives trying to please their earthly fathers or at least get their attention or approval. No matter what your family situation is, God is the perfect Father, and He cares deeply for you. You can find peace in knowing that your heavenly Father is able to meet your needs.

*He Is Our...*

# Hope

*You have been my hope, Sovereign LORD,*
*my confidence since my youth.*

PSALM 71:5

Hope is powerful. It is something we all need. When we feel persecuted for our beliefs, we need hope. When we are discouraged because of life circumstances, we need hope. When we don't know how we will get through tomorrow, we need hope. God is our hope and confidence. He is able to bring new possibilities to even the most impossible circumstances. Place your hope in Him. Remember, faith is being sure of what we hope for and certain of what we do not see.

God is not only our hope, He is also our confidence. He is the one we can place our faith and strength in so that we walk with God-centered, not self-centered, confidence. Placing our hope and confidence in people will leave us needy. Placing our hope in circumstances will leave us unsure. Placing our hope in the Lord is sure, for He loves us and can do all things. Lean on Him. Wait patiently for Him, for He is our hope.

*He Performs...*
# Great Wonders

*You are the God of great wonders!*
*You demonstrate your awesome power among the nations.*
<small>PSALM 77:14 NLT</small>

The laws of nature have no control over the God of wonders. His power rules over all. He demonstrates His awesome power to the nations as He brings victory in battles and dominion over authorities. He places one king on a throne and removes another. He demonstrates His awesome power through the wonders of nature, as we see the strength of a hurricane or the destruction of a tsunami. His deeds command both our fear and our respect.

The God of great wonders also demonstrates His awesome power in our lives personally. He is able to transform a self-centered and hateful sinner into a person filled with love, kindness, compassion, and forgiveness. He shows His power in everyday miracles such as answering prayers for guidance and strength. The God of great wonders can do wonderful things in our lives. Praise Him for His awesome power, and never lose your sense of wonder at what the God of wonders can do in your life.

# Gives Stern Warnings

*Listen to me, O my people, while I give you stern*
*warnings. O Israel, if you would only listen to me!*
PSALM 81:8 NLT

Warning signs on the highway are there for our
own good. When we are warned about road construction, we slow down. If a sign indicates there are
curves ahead, we drive with caution. When we are told,
"Do Not Pass," we are wise to obey. Road warnings help
us make it through life with fewer accidents and colli-
sions.

God had stern warnings for His people because He
loved them and wanted them to experience the joy of
living within His care. Our passage today continues,
"You shall have no foreign god among you; you shall
not worship any god other than me." God warned His
people to remain true to Him and Him alone. The Israelites often strayed from having God in first place in their
hearts. What about us? What or who do we tend to idol-
ize other than God? May this warning serve as a warning to us also. Let us keep our hearts faithful to Him.

# Fills Our Mouths

*Open wide your mouth and I will fill it.*
PSALM 81:10

Have you ever observed a mother bird feeding her young? Safe in their nest, the baby birds open their mouths, and Mama bird distributes food from her mouth. In our passage today, we see God telling His people to "open wide." He wanted to fill their mouths with the portion they needed. He was reassuring them that He would take care of their needs, just as He had in bringing them out of Egypt. Their job was to be open to His kind provision instead of grumbling and complaining.

To fill their mouths meant that He was willing to satisfy their needs. Yet they had to do one thing—open their mouths wide. In other words they needed to look to Him in expectation for His provision. How easily we forget that God wants us to "open wide" and receive from Him.

*Dear Father, our eyes are on You, and we are open to Your comfort and care. Satisfy our hunger both physically and spiritually. Fill us, Father, with Your provision.*

*He Is a...*

# Sun

*The LORD God is a sun and shield.*
PSALM 84:11

There's nothing like the warmth of the sun to take away a winter chill. The light of the sun brings safety as it dispels the darkness and allows us to see clearly. The heat of the sun dries up the soggy mud after a storm. Plants and the fossil fuels that come from them are a product of photosynthesis, getting their energy from the sun. We depend on the sun for earth's life-giving processes.

When you think about the vital role the sun plays in our everyday lives, we can easily see why the psalmist declared, "The LORD God is a sun." He radiates light and love, and our lives depend on Him for provision. He brings healing after a storm, and He sustains our life by nourishing our souls. Without our sun, life on this planet would cease to exist. In a similar way, God is our life, and without Him, life would be dark and meaningless.

*Oh Father, we praise You for the radiance of Your presence in our lives. We glorify You as the giver of life. Thank You for sustaining us and renewing us day by day.*

*He Gives...*

# Favor and Honor

*The LORD bestows favor and honor.*

PSALM 84:11

Our verse today reveals two gifts which the Lord bestows. He is the giver of both favor and honor. The word *favor* means "graciousness or kindness." The same word is used in Proverbs: "He mocks proud mockers but shows favor to the humble and oppressed."[38] Let us humbly come before Him seeking His favor as we live lives that honor Him. The angel reassured Mary, "Do not be afraid...you have found favor with God."[39] What a wonderful gift to be the recipient of God's favor!

He also bestows honor. The psalmist said, "My victory and honor come from God alone."[40] Often we search for our honor from people. It's common to crave attention and recognition. Others live in fear that they may be dishonored or embarrassed. Always remember our true honor comes from the Lord. He protects our honor and guards our reputation as we walk obediently with Him. Trust Him with your honor, and thank Him for bestowing favor upon you.

*He...*

# Withholds No Good Thing

*The LORD will withhold no good thing*
*from those who do what is right.*

PSALM 84:11

God's very nature is kind and good, and because of this He does not withhold His goodness from those who walk uprightly. He gives good gifts. Sometimes things may not seem good at the time. For instance, I remember my mother saying to me, "Eat your vegetables—they are good for you." They didn't seem so good to me at the time, but now I understand. Because Mom loved me, she didn't withhold the vegetables. In a similar way, God knows what is good for us. We must trust He will not withhold anything good from us.

David wrote, "Those who seek the LORD lack no good thing." God did not withhold His only Son. Jesus said, "Seek the kingdom of God above all else, and live righteously, and he will give you everything you need." Knowing Christ and walking with Him is certainly the fulfillment of all good things.

*He Gives...*

# Unfailing Love and Faithfulness

*Your unfailing love will last forever.*
*Your faithfulness is as enduring as the heavens.*
PSALM 89:2 NLT

God's unfailing love and faithfulness go hand in hand. Faithfulness implies steadiness, consistent strength, truth, and stability. God is dependable and consistent. Although people may be unfaithful and undependable, He will never be unfaithful. It is not in His nature. You can trust His love for you. The psalmist declared, "Your love, LORD, reaches to the heavens, your faithfulness to the skies." We cannot begin to fathom the height or depth of God's love and faithfulness. They are limitless!

Our souls find great rest in the unfailing love and faithfulness of the Lord. We do not have to worry about His love running out. It won't. We don't have to worry about His stability or certainty disappearing. It won't. The Bible reassures us of His continued faithfulness. It is one thing to know about God's unfailing love and faithfulness in our minds, but do we trust it with our hearts?

*Father, thank You for Your great and trustworthy love for us.*

# Dwelling Place

*Lord, thou hast been our dwelling-place.*
PSALM 90:1 ASV

When you work with homeless people you recognize the security and dignity that are associated with having a place to stay. Often we take for granted the blessing of having a roof over our heads. Our words today are actually a prayer of Moses, and considered one of the oldest psalms. As Moses and the Israelites wandered in the desert, they had nowhere to call their home. Yet God was all they needed, He was their dwelling place. Their tents in the wilderness were temporary—their God was not.

We have a dwelling place, One whom we can go to for comfort, protection, dignity, and hope. He will not leave us. We are never alone. Moses recognized that God was the One who could meet all their needs. In the New Testament we read Jesus' invitation for us to come and dwell (abide) with Him. We find a home for our restless souls in Him alone.

*Father, thank You for being our dwelling place. We desire to abide with You.*

# Commands His Angels to Guard You

*He will command his angels concerning you*
*to guard you in all your ways.*

PSALM 91:11

Throughout Scripture we read about the work of angels. They have many different jobs and functions in God's kingdom, but one of those roles is to watch over believers. In Hebrews we read, "Angels are only servants—spirits sent to care for people who will inherit salvation." How kind our heavenly Father is to send angels to watch over us. What privileged and blessed children we are! Angels bring glory to God. Psalm 103 says, "Praise the LORD, you his angels, you mighty ones who do his bidding, who obey his word."

We should not live in fear. Nor should we be worried for our loved ones. Instead, remember that God has commanded angels to guard over His own people. Angels serve under God's authority. Do not worship angels or become infatuated by them—rather, thank God for the provision He has sent on our behalf. Rejoice in Him, and trust His care for us.

# Fame Endures

*You, O LORD, will sit on your throne forever.*
*Your fame will endure to every generation.*
PSALM 102:12 NLT

Celebrity fame comes and goes, yet isn't it amazing how people gravitate toward it? Magazines and television shows build their entire focus around celebrity interests and the latest scoop on the Hollywood stars. Even the celebrities are aware that their fame is fleeting and won't last forever. A new generation will bring a new fascination with the latest and greatest stars. If only there were such an interest in the One whose fame never fades. God will sit on His throne forever, and His fame will endure through all generations.

Just as teenagers may pursue the latest heartthrob, we can passionately pursue the most famous One of all. Let us desire to know Him and deliberately seek Him and love Him with all our heart, mind, soul, and strength. His fame will not fade, and His glory will last forever. He is worth our passionate pursuit!

# Listens to the Destitute

*He will listen to the prayers of the destitute.*
*He will not reject their pleas.*

PSALM 102:17 NLT

Those who are destitute have Someone who will listen to them. God listens to their prayers and won't reject their pleas. The word *destitute* not only refers to having physical needs, but also emotional and spiritual ones. Have you ever felt destitute? Poverty of the soul is the common affliction of every man and woman, and this kind of poverty can only be remedied by the Lord.

The Bible reminds us that when we were dead in our sins (spiritually destitute) God made us alive with Christus.[41] God listens to those who come to Him in their spiritual destitution as well as physical or emotional poverty. Let us recognize our need for Him and pour out our hearts and prayers to Him. He can direct us and lead us to the resources we need. He can provide in ways we never thought possible. When we feel poor, we can go to the God of all riches and seek His help and comfort.

*He Is...*

# Always the Same

*They will all wear out like a garment.*
*Like clothing you will change them*
*and they will be discarded.*
*But you remain the same.*
Psalm 102:26-27

Careers change, seasons change, people change—but God remains the same. It's hard to imagine something that doesn't change, yet God's steadiness and unchangeableness brings us security and strength. Although clothing and furniture will wear out over time, He will always remain the same. When the winds of change blow through our lives it is good to know there is an anchor and that we are cared for by a God who remains steadfast and sure.

He will not go away. He will not abandon you or leave you, making you journey through life on your own. He has allowed changes in nature and changes in our lives. They serve as a contrast and point us to the One who does not change. He is the sure foundation for all the changeable things in our lives.

*Thank You, Father, that we can trust You and place our faith in a God who remains.*

# Forgives All Your Sins

*… who forgives all your sins.*
PSALM 103:3

Only God can forgive sin, and He chooses to graciously forgive. We could never pay our debt to the Holy One, but He kindly forgives us all our sins. Christ, the Lamb of God, sacrificed His life, so that once and for all the debt of sin is paid for all who believe.

In Colossians, Paul wrote, "He forgave us all our sins, having canceled the charge of our legal indebtedness, which stood against us and condemned us; he has taken it away, nailing it to the cross."[42] Did you catch the word *all* again? He forgave us *all* our sins. He did not forgive part of our sin or three-quarters of our sin. The word *all* is quite clear. John used the same words when he wrote, "If we confess our sins, he is faithful and just and will forgive us our sins and purify us from *all* unrighteousness."[43]

*Thank You, Father, that our sin, not in part but the whole, has been nailed to the cross and we bear it no more.*

# *He...*
# **Heals Your Diseases**

*... who ... heals all your diseases.*
PSALM 103:3

We all have known someone who has died of an illness, so we wonder what David could mean when he says that God "heals all your diseases." Perhaps you prayed with sincere faith and fervor for someone to be healed, and yet they suffered and died. It's hard to believe David's words when you have faced such heartache. We know beyond a shadow of a doubt that God is able to heal, as we read story after story of healing throughout the Bible.

Still the word *all* tends to bother us. Why doesn't He heal every person every time? We know God chose to allow Paul's thorn in the flesh to remain to show His power through weakness. The truth is everyone dies at some point, whether through illness, accident, or age. The ultimate healing comes after death. The Bible tells us that "he will transform our lowly bodies so they will be like His glorious body."[44] God chooses to heal some people temporarily here on this earth, but ultimately all diseases will be healed in heaven.

# Redeems Your Life

*... who redeems your life from the pit.*
PSALM 103:4

The pit. Been there? There are times in our lives when we simply find ourselves in a rut. It may be an emotional pit of feeling down or blue. It could be a parenting pit, where you find yourself frustrated and worn out. In the job pit, it may seem like you are working endlessly without enough recognition or pay. Maybe you are even in a spiritual pit—a spot where you feel alone. Take heart, my friend. God is a redeeming God, and He is able to redeem your life from the pit.

He can bring new life into those who are worn out with frustrations. Isaiah reminds us that He makes a way through the sea and a path through the mighty waters. When life seems to be at rock bottom, He is able to lift us up. Look up, my friend, whether you are in a pit of your own making or one you didn't choose. Look up and seek Him. He is the God who redeems your life from the pit.

# Crowns You with Love

*... who beautifies, dignifies, and crowns you
with loving-kindness and tender mercy.*

PSALM 103:4 AMP

A crown identifies you as royalty, as someone who is related to the king. As the bride of Christ we have the privilege and honor of being daughters of the King. He beautifies us and dignifies us by crowning us with His loving-kindness and compassion. Let us wear our crown with great joy and thankfulness!

Take a moment right now to close your eyes and picture yourself before the throne of grace. As you bow at His feet, Jesus takes your hand and lifts you up. Then with all the gracious love and tender mercy of our loving God, He places a crown on your head. It looks lovely on you. It serves as a constant reminder of His unfailing love for you. Let your crown be your most important adornment each day. Wear it always, so that all may see in you the joy and confidence of being sincerely loved by the King.

*He...*

# Satisfies Your Desires

*The LORD satisfies your desires with good things*
*so that your youth is renewed like the eagle's.*
PSALM 103:5

God satisfies our desires with His unfailing love, compassionate acceptance, and gracious forgiveness. Our Creator satisfies our soul with good things and fulfills our deepest needs. He fills us up to the point of satisfaction, so that we hunger and thirst no more. Just as our stomachs feel satisfied after a good meal, so our hearts are satisfied as we spend time with Him, feeding on His Word.

As we seek His face and bring our desires before Him we become satisfied. Satisfied in Him, knowing that He will meet all of our needs. He renews our youth like the eagles. Yes, He breathes new life into old worn-out souls! May we continually bring our desires before Him, allowing Him to be our satisfaction and strength. He is good and is able to satisfy us with good things.

# Gives Righteousness and Justice

*The LORD gives righteousness*
*and justice to all who are treated unfairly.*

PSALM 103:6 NLT

Have you been treated unfairly at some time in your life? It may have been in a business transaction, or in your compensation for your work. It may be that someone accused you of doing something you didn't do. Life is filled with unfair moments. It's part of life because we live in a sinful and fallen world. As we learned at an early age, "Life is not fair."

Unfair treatment does not go unnoticed by God. He brings righteousness and justice to all who are oppressed. We can trust that He is at work giving us both righteousness and justice. Paul wrote to the Colossians, "Anyone who does wrong will be repaid for their wrongs, and there is no favoritism."[45] Certainly there are times when we must speak up for the wrong that has been done to us, but let us never forget that God is the one who will bring righteousness and justice.

*He Is...*

# Slow to Anger

*The LORD is compassionate and gracious,*
*slow to anger, abounding in love.*

PSALM 103:8

G od does not rush into anger. He is patient, and He is compassionate, so therefore He is slow to anger. We all know people who have a quick temper and fly off the handle at the smallest provocation, but God is not that way. He does not become angry easily or quickly. Just because He is slow to anger doesn't mean He never gets angry. The Lord's anger burned against the Israelites in the wilderness as they grumbled and failed to trust Him. The prophets warned of His wrath if His people continued to turn away from Him. Yet even then He said, "I will not be angry forever."

God is extravagant when it comes to compassion and grace, yet He is very stingy when it comes to anger. He holds it back, He waits, and He does not expend it often or flagrantly. Even His anger is grounded in love, as His deepest desire is for all to know Him and follow Him.

# Does Not Always Accuse

*He will not always accuse,*
*nor will he harbor his anger forever.*

PSALM 103:9

There is an accuser, but it is not our God. Satan is called the accuser, and he is constantly accusing us in our minds. He reminds us of our mistakes and brings up our past sins, wanting us to forget that our loving heavenly Father is patient with us. Satan wants us to think God is always angry with us, but our verse today reminds us that our dear Father does not harbor His anger forever. He is not like the accuser.

God is not a bitter and angry deity; rather, He is redeeming and loving. He does not hold onto the past like we do. Sadly, we tend to replay past hurts that make us bitter and angry. It's hard for us to imagine that God isn't like us. He doesn't harbor His anger forever. Let us seek His help to be more like Him. May we live with love and forgiveness as He does and no longer hold on to our anger.

# Does Not Deal Harshly with Us

*He does not deal harshly with us, as we deserve.*

PSALM 103:10 NLT

This truth alone should make us live in gratitude every day of our lives. *Thank You, Father, that You do not treat us as we deserve. Thank You, Lord, that You do not deal harshly with us!* If God chose to discipline and punish us for all our sins, we would all be dead! Yet God is patient with us. The Bible tells us that He does discipline us at times as a loving Father, but we are reassured that He doesn't punish us for all our sins nor does He deal harshly with us.

God knows we are works in progress. In Philippians we learn, "He who began a good work in you will carry it on to completion until the day of Christ Jesus." He is patient and understanding of our weaknesses. He doesn't give up on us when we make a wrong turn or bad choice or mistake, or when we sin. He is long-suffering with us. Because we are recipients of such grace, shouldn't we show this type of patience and forbearance toward others?

# Love Is Great

*As high as the heavens are above the earth,
so great is his love for those who fear him.*

PSALM 103:11

Endless! Immeasurable! Vast! Indescribable! Beyond what we can see! That's how high the heavens are above the earth, and that's the way David described God's love toward us. Those who fear Him are loved with a love so great that it is truly undefinable. Take a moment to ponder and breathe in God's great love for you. The enemy wants you to forget how much you are loved by your Father, so we must reflect each day on how dearly loved we are. Thank Him for His love right now.

It's hard to imagine how long and wide and high and deep the love of Christ is for His followers. Christ showed His great love for us by offering His life on our behalf. We didn't deserve it, but His love for us is so great that He willingly offered to suffer and die for us. How can anyone ignore a love so great? Walk in His love. Dwell on it, think on it, allow it to permeate your life.

# Removes Our Transgressions

*As far as the east is from the west,*
*so far has he removed our transgressions from us.*

PSALM 103:12

Have you ever spilled something red on a white outfit? You probably remember the frustration of trying to get the stain out and hoping you hadn't ruined your clothing. In a spiritual sense, sin stains each of our lives. The Bible says there is not one person who is righteous, not one. But there is One who can remove our stain. Through Christ our transgressions are removed. Because of the cross we can stand clean before a Holy God.

How far is the east from the west? The distance cannot be measured. That's how far He has removed our transgressions from us. They are gone. He does not retrieve them to dwell on them. He removes them completely. Remember this the next time you start retrieving your own transgressions in your mind. It is gone; the stain is removed. Do not try to bring it back, and don't try to bring up the past sins of others either.

# Compassion Like a Father

*As a father has compassion on his children,*
*so the LORD has compassion on those who fear him.*

PSALM 103:13

Picture a loving father holding a newborn baby girl. He adores her and is filled with love for his precious and fragile child. He wants the best for her and desires to help her as she grows and becomes a young lady. God our Father tenderly holds us in His arms with the compassion of a loving father. The verb form of *compassion* in the Hebrew actually means "to be merciful or show pity" on someone.

Babies are helpless. They can't feed themselves or nurture themselves. Someone must have mercy and take pity upon them to help them survive. Just as a strong father looks at the tiny child in His arms, so the Lord sees our needs and offers His care. God shows His tender mercies toward us each day as His children. Even if you did not have a faithful and loving father on this earth, you can know you have a heavenly Father who loves you and cares for you.

*He...*

# Knows How We Are Formed

*He knows how we are formed,*
*he remembers that we are dust.*

Psalm 103:14

God is not surprised by our mistakes or shocked by our human nature. He understands our temperament and personality. He is not confused by our appearance, nor is He scratching His head wondering why we have certain differences or quirks. He knows how we were formed, and He understands all there is to know about us. He knows us better than we know ourselves. He told Jeremiah, "Before I formed you in the womb I knew you, before you were born I set you apart."[46]

David wrote,

> You created my inmost being, you knit me together in my mother's womb. I praise you because I am fearfully and wonderfully made; your works are wonderful, I know that full well. My frame was not hidden from you when I was made in the secret place. When I was woven together in the depths of the earth, your eyes saw my unformed body.[47]

God knows us through and through and is understanding toward us. He knows that we sin and that's why He sent a Savior.

*He Is...*

# Clothed with Splendor and Majesty

*You are clothed with splendor and majesty.*
*The LORD wraps himself in light as with a garment.*
PSALM 104:1-2

In some ways our clothing defines us. What we choose to wear shows the people around us something about our interests and our tastes. Clothing often reveals our occupation. Those in the medical field are identified by their scrubs and lab coats. Policemen, firemen, and service professionals are often recognized by their official uniforms. God's clothing identifies His character as well, yet His clothing is nothing like human clothing. He is clothed with splendor and majesty too brilliant to take in.

Splendor and majesty imply overwhelming beauty, glory, and dignity. David poetically described the magnificence of the Lord. Brilliant light surrounds Him—He is too wonderful to behold. It is beyond our imagination to picture His clothing, overwhelming with beauty and splendor and wrapped in light. *Praise You, most holy God. You are beautiful and magnificent.*

*He...*

# Made Variety in Creation

*O LORD, what a variety of things you have made!*
*In wisdom you have made them all.*

PSALM 104:24 NLT

Aren't you glad when you go to buy ice cream that vanilla isn't the only flavor? Aren't you thankful when you go to a restaurant that there is more than one item on the menu? Isn't it good to be able to choose from more than one sample of wallpaper? Without variety, life would be dull! In our passage today, the psalmist is rejoicing over the variety God has placed in nature. He fashioned and created an immense bounty of plants and animals in a marvelous array of colors.

In wisdom He created a variety of people as well. I'm so glad we are not all alike. He's given us different looks, different personalities, different gifts and talents. It's funny how we can get so annoyed at the differences in others ... as if we expected everyone to be just like us. Let's learn to rejoice in the differences and recognize that variety in people makes this world an interesting place. No one is exactly like you. Celebrate the variety of creation today, not expecting everyone to be like you.

# Takes Pleasure in All He Has Made

*The LORD takes pleasure in all he has made!*
PSALM 104:31 NLT

God takes pleasure in His creation. He finds great joy and delight in the work of His hands. He enjoys the beauty He has created in this world. He takes pleasure in the plants and the animals, the sky and the sea, and in us! What an amazing thought. He delights in interacting with us. He doesn't become annoyed when we call out to Him; rather, He smiles and is glad that we come to Him.

If the Creator of all things takes pleasure in what He has created, shouldn't we do so as well? The Gnostic philosophers believed that matter was evil and therefore one should be detached from it. But God created this world for Himself and for us to enjoy. Now we must be careful not to worship or misuse what He has created. Let us instead take delight in the work of His hands.

*Father, thank You for all You have created. We take pleasure in the work of Your hands just as You do.*

*He Has Done...*

# Marvelous Works

*Remember His marvelous works which He has done,*
*His wonders, and the judgments of His mouth.*
PSALM 105:5 NKJV

There are some things in life that are best forgotten. We need to steer clear of reflecting and dwelling on past hurts or mistakes or grievances, so that anger or bitterness will not grip our hearts and minds. Just as there are things we should forget, there are some things we should remember. We should remember God's marvelous works and the wonderful things He has done in our lives. We should reflect on the times He has been faithful and kind to us.

When the Israelites entered the Promised Land they were specifically instructed by God to remember all the things He had done for them. Sadly, they soon forgot His wonders and went back to grumbling and complaining. We also have a choice. We can forget God's kindness as we grumble and complain, or we can reflect on all His blessings and trust His goodness. Let us be deliberate about remembering God's wonderful works as well as His judgments. He is marvelous and does marvelous works each day of our lives.

*He Has Performed...*

# Innumerable Miracles

*Who can list the glorious miracles of the LORD?*
PSALM 106:2 NLT

The apostle John closed his Gospel by declaring, "Jesus did many other things as well. If every one of them were written down I suppose that even the whole world would not have room for the books that would be written." The glorious miracles of the Lord are too numerous to count. If we were going to make a list beginning with creation in Genesis and proceeding through the Bible, we would become literally overwhelmed by the task.

Sometimes we look for the big dramatic miracles like the ones in the Bible, and we overlook the ones God does in our life each day. Consider the miracle of a baby's birth. Or the miracle of a butterfly. Or the miracle of a beautiful sunset, or the miracle that we are able to see, hear, feel, touch, and taste. Don't take anything for granted. Open your eyes and see the miracles around you. Your fears will diminish while your faith grows.

*He...*

# Deserves Unending Praise

*Who can ever praise him enough?*
PSALM 106:2 NLT

We can never run out of reasons to praise the Lord. He alone is worthy of continual praise, for He alone is perfect in every way. David wrote, "I will extol the LORD at all times; his praise will always be on my lips." Paul said, "Rejoice in the Lord always." Praising God honors His name and changes our outlook on life. It is usually easy to praise Him when times are good and things are going well in our lives, although often we forget to praise Him even then. Yet if we will praise Him in the midst of our struggles, we will see life from a whole different perspective.

What exactly does it mean to praise the Lord? It means to bring honor to Him and recognize who He is. Praise is turning our eyes upward and gazing upon the glorious Lord and all His wonderful attributes. It may be speaking, singing, or thinking about all He is and all He has done. Certainly, when we focus on the Lord, we recognize we can never praise Him enough.

# **Continues to Rescue**

*Again and again he rescued them.*
Psalm 106:43 nlt

God did not just simply rescue His people once. He rescued them over and over again. In the Old Testament we see a pattern with the Israelites: They rebelled against the Lord, He sent punishment, they cried out to Him, He rescued them. We see His kindness and compassion displayed through His willingness to rescue His people when they were in despair. But the passage goes on to say they were finally destroyed by their sin. Although the Lord rescued again and again, He finally allowed them to be the victims of their own sin. May we never test the Lord's patience to the extent that He allows us to self-destruct because of our own evil behavior.

God is a compassionate Father. Even those who rebel find mercy when they turn to Him. He is a rescuer to those who turn away from sin and turn toward Him. There is hope for those who have messed up more than a time or two! Turn to Him, for His compassion is abundant.

# Pities Those in Distress

*He pitied them in their distress
and listened to their cries.*
PSALM 106:44 NLT

When the Israelites found themselves in distress as a result of their own rebellion, God pitied them and listened to their cries. He did not turn a deaf ear and forget about them even when they forgot about Him. His kindness reached beyond their rebellion. There is great comfort in this verse, as we see that we can come to God with our cares and troubles even if we have brought them on ourselves.

Sin, rebellion, and bad choices often result in challenges and troubles in our life. It's easy to feel guilty and want to cower and hide instead of bringing our needs before the Lord in our lowest moments. Although walking in His ways is always best, it is important to know that we can repent and call to God, who pities us in our distress. He may not smooth out all our troubles, but we know that He listens to our cries and will not forsake us.

# Relents

*For their sake he remembered his covenant*
*and out of his great love he relented.*

Psalm 106:45

God relented on His punishment toward His people, not because they deserved it, but because His love and mercy are so very great. The word for "relented" in this passage actually means "a strong turning toward a new and positive course of action, to exert strength, to change, to re-grasp the situation." Like someone pulling back on the reins of a horse that is galloping full speed in one direction, so He pulled back and turned His anger away from His people.

Despite the fact that God relented on His punishment, there is one area where He does not relent. God is unrelenting when it comes to His love for us. He does not give up on us, even though we may take our eyes off of Him. Thankfully, God is relenting when it comes to the consequences we deserve, but He is unrelenting and unchanging when it comes to the love we don't deserve.

# Satisfies the Thirsty

*He satisfies the thirsty and fills the
hungry with good things.*
PSALM 107:9

What does your soul thirst for? What seems to be the deep desire that gnaws like a hunger in your heart? Although we all seem to have an innate need to feel loved and accepted, there exists a greater hunger and thirst within us: to know God and feel loved and accepted by Him. The psalmist wrote, "As the deer pants for streams of water, so my soul pants for you, my God. My soul thirsts for God, for the living God."[48] In the depths of our hearts there is a great need and desire to know the One who created us and will love us with a true, faithful, and unconditional love.

Our soul can only be satisfied by a relationship with the living God. He fills up our emptiness with His completeness and love. He brings fulfillment and satisfaction to those who hunger and thirst after Him. They will not be disappointed.

*Father, thank You that we are complete and filled up in You. You satisfy our deepest longing.*

# Brings Us out of Darkness

*He brought them out of darkness, the utter darkness.*
PSALM 107:14

Have you ever been in a place of utter darkness? As a young girl I toured a cave in Central Texas. The guides took us deep into the cave where there was no hint of outside light. For a moment they turned off the lights, and we experienced complete darkness. I'd much rather be in the light than dwell in utter darkness. God brings us out of darkness. When His light shines in our lives, we no longer stumble around blinded by darkness.

He brings the light of salvation, so that we are set free from the darkness of sin and death. His Word gives light to our pathway, so that we can see where to go and how to live. He lights up our hearts with His love, so that we can freely love others. He sheds light on our sin, so we can repent and move forward in the freedom He brings. Let us walk in the light as He is in the light each day.

*He...*

# Breaks Down Prison Bars

*He broke down their prison gates of bronze;*
*he cut apart their bars of iron.*
PSALM 107:16

Although we may not have prison bars surrounding us, there are times when we may feel held captive by our circumstances. It may be a job that seems to imprison you. Or perhaps you feel isolated as a mom at home with kids. Maybe you feel all alone in your neighborhood, or you are held captive by an illness or handicap. If God can break down prison gates and cut apart bars of iron, He can do miraculous things through your captivity as well.

He may not break down the gates by changing your circumstances, but He can give you joy and hope in the midst of them. He can give you a new perspective and fresh possibilities to use your captivity for a greater purpose. Remember, the prison bars did not stop Paul from writing and proclaiming the gospel. Prison bars have no strength against a great and powerful God.

*He...*

# Calms the Storms

*He calmed the storm to a whisper*
*and stilled the waves.*
PSALM 107:29 NLT

It's amazing how quickly a severe storm in life can develop. Just when we thought life was rowing merrily along, a storm hits with gale-force winds, and we have no control over our own situation. Yet God is able to calm our storm to a whisper and still the waves. He is able to bring us safely into the harbor.

The disciples had the opportunity to experience God's calming power firsthand. While Jesus slept in the boat, the disciples fought the waves and feared for their lives. Finally they woke Jesus up and asked for His help. He spoke and calmed the sea. He showed His power over nature by this miracle. Jesus is in the boat with us. Go to Him and seek His help. Allow Him to calm your fears and bring a blessed stillness to your restless thoughts.

*His...*

# Love Is Higher than the Heavens

*Great is your love, higher than the heavens;*
*your faithfulness reaches to the skies.*

PSALM 108:4

When you picture almighty God, what comes to mind? Often we think of Him as an angry or frustrated heavenly parent looking down at us with disappointment or disgust. Yet that is not who He is. He is abounding in love and rich in mercy. His love is higher than the heavens.

Certainly we must revere His holiness and stand in awe at His greatness. But we must also reflect on His great and limitless love for us. In the New Testament we read Paul's prayer for the believers: "I pray that you ... may have power, together with all the Lord's holy people, to grasp how wide and long and high and deep is the love of Christ, and to know this love that surpasses knowledge."[49] Paul also reminded us that nothing can separate us from the love of Christ. Let us walk confidently in His great love for us. May it overflow from our hearts to touch the lives of many through our words and actions.

# Helps Us to Do Mighty Things

*With God's help we will do mighty things.*
PSALM 108:13 NLT

He helps us to do things we could never dream of doing on our own. Certainly David knew this first-hand when he slew the giant Goliath with just a sling-shot and a stone. In our own power and strength, we are limited. Mighty things are accomplished when we seek God and allow Him to work through us. In other translations of the Scriptures the word *valiantly* is used for "mighty things." Through God we will do valiantly—we will move forward victoriously with strength and power.

Why do we try to do things in our own strength, without seeking His help? Why do we forge ahead without Him? Consider your life right now. Are there areas where you need to seek His help and guidance? With His help you can do valiantly; without Him you are on your own. Seek His help and join with Him. Allow Him to work powerfully through you today.

# Stands Beside the Needy

*He stands beside the needy, ready to save
them from those who condemn them.*

PSALM 109:31 NLT

I t seems that there is never a shortage of people who
flock toward the rich and famous. But the needy?
Well, probably not so many! Most people tend to keep
their distance from the needy because they can be
demanding of time, effort, and money. Yet God does
not run from those in need—rather, He comes to their
aid. He stands beside them and is ready to defend them.

If we are going to be perfectly honest, aren't we all
needy to some extent? Some may be needy emotionally,
while others have physical needs or financial worries.
The bottom line is, we all need Him. We can take comfort from our passage today that He is close beside us.
We can also be inspired by the Lord's example to stand
by the needy. Let us seek His guidance and strength as
to how we can make a difference in the life of someone in need.

# Works Reveal His Glory

*Everything he does reveals his glory and majesty.*
PSALM 111:3 NLT

Everything God has done, all of His works, reveal His great glory. We see it everywhere. The heavens declare the glory of God. The skies proclaim the works of His hands. Those who want to see God's majesty and greatness need only to open their eyes to the world around them and see God's handiwork in everything He has done. His wisdom and goodness are evident in every flower in the field and every drop of rain from the sky.

It's hard to imagine anyone truthfully saying, "I just didn't realize there is a God." The evidence of God's glory is too obvious to ignore. In Romans we read,

> Ever since the world was created, people have seen the earth and sky. Through everything God made, they can clearly see his invisible qualities— his eternal power and divine nature. So they have no excuse for not knowing God. [50]

God has set His signature in creation. It speaks for itself.

*There Is...*

# No One Like Him

*Who is like the LORD our God?*
PSALM 113:5

It's tempting to compare God's characteristics to human qualities. We compare His compassion to the compassion we see in a particular person. We may picture His mercy as being like that of a merciful individual we know. Often we think of His anger as something like the anger of a mean parent or disgruntled boss. But God is not like us. He has no flaws. His character is not blemished with sin or self-centeredness.

There is no one who can even come close to being worthy of comparison to God. His mercy is beyond what we can imagine. His compassion and unfailing love are immeasurable. Even His anger is a pure and righteous anger, and is infused with both mercy and justice. He is completely unique and is like no one. All praise to Him, for no one is like the Almighty Lord.

*He...*

# Stoops Down

*The One who sits enthroned on high...*
*stoops down to look on the heavens and the earth.*
PSALM 113:5-6

It is an amazing and humbling thought to realize that the Lord God Almighty, who sits enthroned on high, stoops down to look toward us. He loves us and cares for our needs. He is not too haughty or high and mighty to think about us. No, the High King of heaven bends down to watch over His people. What comfort to know that He acts on our behalf!

When we consider the greatness of our glorious Lord and think about Him stooping to care for us, it makes us recognize we have no right or room to think of ourselves too highly to help another in need. Ask the High King of heaven, who stoops down to look at us, to open your eyes to see the needs around you today.

# Deliverer

*You, O LORD, have delivered my soul from death,*
*my eyes from tears, my feet from stumbling.*

PSALM 116:8

Oh, what a wonderful deliverer the Lord is in our lives! He is the only one who can deliver our souls from death. Christ is the One whom God sent to deliver us from our sin problem. God also delivers our eyes from tears. Notice that it doesn't say we will have no tears, but He delivers us from those tears. He dries our eyes with His presence and peace as He walks with us through difficulties or heartaches.

He delivers our feet from stumbling. We may walk through rocky paths, but He keeps us from stumbling. The Bible reminds us that if we stumble we will not fall, for the Lord holds us by the hand.[51] Just as the Israelites looked to Him as their deliverer from slavery, so our eyes are on the Lord our Deliverer to guide us through and rescue us from the challenges we face in life.

*He Is Our...*

# Hiding Place

*You are my hiding place and my shield.*
PSALM 119:114 NKJV

Hide-and-seek was one of my favorite games as a child. I loved the challenge of finding the "perfect hiding spot." No matter how creative I was, eventually I was always found. There is only one perfect "hiding place," and that is in the arms of the Lord. In the New Testament we read that "our lives are hidden with Christ in God."[52] In Christ, we cannot be reached by the enemy.

The word *hidden* means concealed and safe. We are safe in God's arms both now and for the future. Right now we can trust that whatever happens to us, His loving arms will hold us, and He will see us through. Only what He has permitted will enter our lives, for we are safely hidden in Him. We are also hidden safely in His arms when it comes to our eternal destiny. No one can snatch believers in Christ from His arms.[53] We are sealed for the day of redemption[54] and hidden in Him.

*He Is...*

# Near

*You are near, O LORD,*
*and all your commands are true.*
PSALM 119:151

The Lord is not far away; He is close. He is near. What comfort that is when we feel alone or afraid. He is our constant companion, our comforter and present help in time of need. When you find yourself being tossed about by the waves in the storm of life, remember that God is near. He is in the boat with you. When you find yourself walking through the darkest valleys, do not be afraid, for your Shepherd is close beside you.

Sometimes He may not feel near, but His presence is not based on our feelings. When we do not feel the warmth of the sun, it doesn't mean that it is not present. When we don't feel the warmth of His love, it doesn't mean that He is not there. Trust the words of the psalmist, who experienced both great joy and great heartache, God is near. His presence is sure, and His word is true.

*He Is Our...*

# Help

*My help comes from the LORD,*
*the Maker of heaven and earth.*

PSALM 121:2

David looked to the hills and declared that his help
came from the Lord. Other nations looked to
the hills because that's where they believed their pagan
gods dwelt. Can't you just see David looking to the hills
as he was watching his flock and thinking to himself, *The
pagans look to the hills for their help, but I look to the Maker
of the hills for mine?* Where do you look for your help?

When we find ourselves in the midst of a challenge
of any kind, we have a choice. We can fret and worry and
look for help from a myriad of sources, or we can go to
the God who created all things and seek His help and
direction. He can lead us to the help we need; He may
bring help to us in a variety of ways. He is a very present help in time of need.

*He...*

# Watches Over You

*He will not let your foot slip—*
*he who watches over you will not slumber.*

PSALM 121:3

When we are sleeping, He is not. His eyes are on us day and night, for our loving heavenly Father continually watches over us. There is great peace in knowing we are never alone. God, who made both the heavens and the earth, watches over us with tender care. We can take comfort in knowing His all-seeing eyes are gracious and full of compassion. The One who watches over us overflows with mercy and loves to care for His own.

God does not fall asleep, like an exhausted watch guard. He is always awake and alert. He is not surprised by the challenges we face, for He sees all. His eyes do not turn away from us, nor do they close in slumber while we struggle through heartache or pain. His eyes are wide open. He guides our feet through the difficulties and won't let them slip as we trudge through the storm. We are in good hands, because our Maker is also our Keeper!

*He...*

# Keeps No Record of Our Sins

*If you, O Lord, kept a record of sins, O Lord,
who could stand? But with you there is forgiveness.*

Psalm 130:3-4

If God kept a tally of our sins, we would all be hopeless. But we are reminded in our passage today that He is the God of forgiveness. He holds forgiveness in His hands, and He is to be feared and reverenced. Just as we would go before a judge with a humble reverence, recognizing his power to acquit or condemn, so also do we approach the Judge of all the earth with respect.

Because of what Christ did on the cross we are without blemish and free from accusation. His followers are pardoned from their sins, set free, with no list or tally remaining. On the other hand, those who reject Him will face judgment for their sins. With Christ there is forgiveness and mercy. May we live each day in humble gratitude.

# Faithful Love Endures Forever

*His faithful love endures forever.*
PSALM 136:1

It is difficult to adequately describe what is meant by the term "faithful love." Some translations use the words *mercy* or *gracious love* to describe it. In the original Hebrew the word is *chesed,* and it is considered one of the most important terms in Old Testament theology and ethics. There are three basic meanings of the word that always interact together: *strength, steadfastness,* and *love.* The term loses its richness and strength if we fail to recognize all three meanings together.

*Love* may seem like a sentimental term, but when we put it together with *steadfastness* and *strength* we understand the enduring power of God's great and gracious love for us. *Chesed* is a word that implies not only loyalty; it also implies mercy. Those who are strong show mercy (*chesed*) toward those who are weak, providing protection and provision. Let us rejoice continually as we reflect on God's faithful and enduring love—His *chesed*—toward us.

*He Is...*

# Everywhere

*Where can I go from your Spirit?*
*Where can I flee from your presence?*
PSALM 139:7

You can't hide from God. One of the beautiful qualities about God is that He is omnipresent. Everywhere. You can't go anywhere that He doesn't see your situation and know your needs. How wonderful it is to know that we are never alone! David proclaimed God's presence in the wings of the dawn and the far side of the sea...even there His hand will guide us and His right hand will hold us. We are never fenced off or separated from His loving presence.

Jonah tried to run from God, but he couldn't escape God's presence even in the belly of the whale. "From inside the fish Jonah prayed to the LORD his God. He said: 'In my distress I called to the LORD, and he answered me. From deep in the realm of the dead I called for help, and you listened to my cry.'"[55] I like what Corrie ten Boom said: "There is no pit so deep that God's love is not deeper still."

*Thank You, Father, that we are never out of Your reach.*

# Refuge for the Righteous

*The way of the LORD is a refuge for the righteous,*
*But it is the ruin of those who do evil.*

PROVERBS 10:29

David proclaimed that God is our refuge, but Solomon said that the *way* of the Lord is a refuge for the righteous. God Himself is not only a fortress and a stronghold for His people, but His ways also provide refuge and strength. What do we mean by the way of the Lord? The term implies everything that He does— His works, His actions, and His commands. The way of the Lord defines who He is by what He does. His ways and works provide protection, joy, and peace for the righteous.

Those who do evil do not find such comfort. Because God's ways are just and righteous, those who choose to do evil will only come to ruin. They will be destroyed because of their own choices. The consequences of their actions will ultimately bring them to destruction. We can choose to take refuge in the ways of the Lord, or we can go our own way.

*He Is...*

# Watching Everywhere

*The Lord is watching everywhere,
keeping his eye on both the evil and the good.*
PROVERBS 15:3 NLT

When we hear about terrible evil in this world, our tendency is to question whether God is watching. It's hard to think that He could see evil and injustice but not zap and destroy it right there. But we are not God and don't understand His ways. If He were to send down lightning to strike every bit of evil on this earth, then the world would have been burned up a long time ago. His patience endures, even in allowing evil to play out.

We can be assured through our passage today that God is watching everywhere. Nothing is hidden from His eyes. He sees both the evil and the good on this earth. Scripture tells us that the Lord is against those who do evil.[56] We must trust His righteous judgment and justice. He is watching, and He will bring justice in due time. Do not fret because of evildoers—rather, live in a way to honor Him since you know He is watching.

# Detests the Way of the Wicked

*The LORD detests the way of the wicked
but he loves those who pursue righteousness.*

PROVERBS 15:9

God can't stand the deeds of the wicked. He hates the effect wickedness has on people's lives. In His kindness God gave us a free will so we might choose the righteous path, but many choose the wicked way. He didn't program us all to be obedient children, like little robots. We know He allows the wicked to make their choices, but He also knows their fate. The Bible reminds us that the wicked will face judgment.

I'd rather be the person who pursues righteousness. God loves those who choose His path and walk in His ways. He delights in those who run toward what is right and good. Let us be people who pursue (actively hunt for) righteousness and live it out in our lives day by day. The pursuit of righteousness ultimately leads us to the cross, where we recognize that through faith in Christ we are clothed with His righteousness.

*Father, thank You for the cross, so that even the wicked may find redemption as they turn to You.*

*He...*

# Tears Down the Proud

*The LORD tears down the proud man's house.*
**PROVERBS 15:25**

Normally we think of God as the Creator and the One who builds up, not tears down. Yet our passage today tells us that He tears down the proud man's house. We see this in the story of the Tower of Babel, when God tore down those who had lifted themselves up to try to challenge Him. We also observe the way He handled the proud when we read the story of King Belshazzar, who saw the handwriting on the wall. Due to his own pride his kingdom was destroyed.

In the New Testament Peter warns, "'God opposes the proud but gives grace to the humble.' Humble yourselves, therefore, under God's mighty hand, that he may lift you up in due time." Humility is a beautiful quality. Humble people recognize that all they have comes from God, and they use it willingly to serve and build up others, not themselves. Let us guard our hearts from pride and bring glory to God through using the gifts He has given us.

# Honest Scales

*Honest scales and balances belong to the LORD.*
PROVERBS 16:11

G od sets the standard for honest scales. In Proverbs we also read, "The LORD detests dishonest scales, but accurate weights find favor with him."[57] God is honest and just, and He wants us to be honest and just as well. There are temptations all around us to be dishonest, both in personal life and business. Subtle temptations often arise to be unjust to others for our own selfish gain. Even gossip can be a dishonest scale by which we judge others unjustly.

It takes discernment, wisdom, and courage to do the right thing. God delights in the truth, but He detests a lying tongue or a false witness who pours out lies. Let us go to the Father, asking Him to open our eyes to the dishonesty that lurks in our hearts. Seek His guidance in always being honest and just with others.

*He Is a...*

# Strong Tower

*The name of the LORD is a fortified tower;*
*the righteous run to it and are safe.*

PROVERBS 18:10

When challenges or opportunities come our way, our thoughts often turn toward worry and fear and dwelling on what-if scenarios. Where should we let our minds run? The name of the Lord is a strong and fortified tower. We can run to Him and find protection, shelter, safety, and well-being.

In Solomon's day, a fortified tower was a place people could run to in order to be protected from an enemy. A tower provides not only safety but elevation above attackers, giving the people inside an advantage over their foes. When Satan tempts us with sin, doubt, and discouragement, we can run to the Lord, our strong tower, for security and victory over our enemy. As we abide in the tower of the Lord we have a better vantage point to look at our circumstances with a broader, more eternal view. Run to God—He is our immovable tower of refuge and strength.

# Searches Our Inmost Being

*The LORD's light penetrates the human spirit,*
*exposing every hidden motive.*
PROVERBS 20:27 NLT

God is interested in what is going on in our inmost being, and He intentionally searches there. Our motives and desires are not hidden from Him. He knows and cares about our spirit and what is in our heart of hearts. David said, "Who can discern his errors? Forgive my hidden faults."[58] David knew that since he couldn't see his own hidden faults, he needed to ask God to reveal them.

Knowing that God sees the things about me that I cannot see about myself makes me realize my need to stay close to Him. I need Him to do the deep cleaning in my inmost being, the dark places that no one knows. As we desire to sincerely serve God and live with pure motives, we shouldn't just clean up the surface stuff. Ask God to do a deep cleansing, so that we may say with David, "May the words of my mouth and the meditation of my heart be pleasing in your sight, O LORD."

*He...*

# Gives Sight

*The poor and the oppressor have this in common:*
*The LORD gives sight to the eyes of both.*
PROVERBS 29:13

It is God who illuminates our eyes. Certainly He is the one who allows us to have physical sight, but He also opens our eyes to spiritual wisdom and insight. Jesus referred to the Pharisees as "blind guides" because they led people into spiritual darkness instead of pointing them to the light. Although they could see physically, they were spiritually blind to the Messiah.

Jesus also quoted Isaiah's warning about spiritual blindness: "The hearts of these people are hardened... they have closed their eyes—so their eyes cannot see... and their hearts cannot understand, and they cannot turn to me and let me heal them."[59] God heals our spiritual blindness. If you don't know where to go or cannot see the hope ahead of you, ask the Father who gives sight to the eyes to illuminate your heart and mind so that you can see His truth more clearly.

*He Is...*

# Exalted

*I saw the LORD sitting on a throne, high and lifted up, and the train of His robe filled the temple.*
ISAIAH 6:1 NKJV

Isaiah had the privilege of seeing the Lord high and lifted up, exalted on His throne. In his vision he saw angels above the throne calling to one another, "Holy, holy, holy *is* the LORD of hosts; The whole earth is full of His glory!" The greatness, power, and holiness of the Lord so awed Isaiah that he cried out, "Woe is me, for I am undone! Because I am a man of unclean lips ... For my eyes have seen the King, the LORD of hosts."

When we consider the majesty of the Lord, we can't help but be affected. He is the Exalted One. As we lift Him up in our hearts, we recognize our own sin and unworthiness. Just like Isaiah, when we consider God's glory and excellence we see our need for His mercy and grace.

*Father, we exalt You, for You alone are worthy of praise. We recognize our sin and our need for a savior. Thank You for the blood of Christ, which purifies our sins.*

*He Is…*

# Immanuel

*The virgin will conceive and give birth to a son,*
*and will call him Immanuel.*

ISAIAH 7:14

Immanuel—God with us! How can it be that He would leave His throne in heaven and dwell among men? God in the flesh. God among us. Jesus is the fulfillment of this prophecy from Isaiah. He humbly came to be with us, leaving His throne and place of honor in heaven in order to dwell among us and eventually die on our behalf.

God is still with us in the form of His Spirit, who dwells within every follower of Christ. In the Old Testament God dwelt among His people in a place known as the Holy of Holies in the temple. Now He dwells in the hearts of those who believe in Christ. God is not a distant God; He is with us.

*Father, we are filled with joy because we know You have chosen to be with us and dwell among us. We rejoice in Your presence in our lives.*

*He Is the...*

# Prince of Peace

*His name shall be called Wonderful, Counselor,*
*Mighty God, Everlasting Father, Prince of Peace.*
ISAIAH 9:6 ASV

We have learned about the God of peace, but today we consider the Prince of Peace, Jesus. Isaiah's prophecy about Jesus reminds us that the God of peace has sent His Son to bring peace between God and man. He did not come to bring world peace, for even Jesus said, "These things have I spoken unto you, that in me ye may have peace. In the world ye have tribulation: but be of good cheer; I have overcome the world."[60]

At the birth of Jesus the angels proclaimed, "Glory to God in the highest, and on earth peace among men in whom he is well pleased."[61] The Prince of Peace had been born. In Romans we read, "Being...justified by faith, we have peace with God through our Lord Jesus Christ."[62] We may not have peace in this world, but we have peace with God through the Prince of Peace, Jesus.

*He Does Everything with...*
# Zeal

*The zeal of the L<small>ORD</small> Almighty will accomplish this.*
I<small>SAIAH</small> 9:7

To work *zealously* for a cause we believe in means to work fervently with strength, perseverance, focus, and power. *Zeal* is a strong word, one that requires an objective. God's zeal was for His people. He passionately desired to redeem them and bring them back to Himself. We see in our previous passage (Isaiah 9:6) that God promised the Prince of Peace to bring peace between God and man. In this verse, we read how He will accomplish it. The zeal of the Lord Almighty will do it. God's passion to redeem His people will bring about His promise of His Son.

God had great zeal for His people in the Old Testament, and His zeal never fades. "His goodness and unfailing love pursue us all the days of our lives," wrote David. What do you and I zealously and fervently pursue? What does our zeal accomplish? God's zeal accomplished redemption for all who believe. May our zeal for God bring about a deeper love relationship with Him.

*He...*

# Wipes Away Our Tears

*The Sovereign LORD will wipe
away the tears from all faces.*
ISAIAH 25:8

Weeping may endure for a night, but joy comes with the morning light. Here on this earth we experience tears and sorrow. We know pain and sadness in this life, but we also know that one day God will wipe every tear away. Suffering makes us long for something better and reminds us that this world is not all there is. We have wonderful joy to look forward to in the presence of our Father. He will dry the tears from our faces as we enter His presence.

He cares about our sorrows, for He is the God of all comfort. He brings us comfort in our troubles here and now. The truth is, we will continue to experience tears until that glorious day in His presence. Tears make us human, but they also serve as a reminder of a better day when He will wipe them all away.

# Upright One

*The path of the righteous is level; you, the Upright
One, make the way of the righteous smooth.*

ISAIAH 26:7

God is the only one who deserves the title "Upright
One." The Bible reminds us that there is no one
righteous, not a single one. As the one and only righteous one, God stands in the category alone. He embodies righteousness, holiness, and purity. There is no guile
in Him. He demonstrates righteousness in all of His
works and actions. He can do no wrong.

The Israelites typically designated a good road for
traveling as a "level road," as opposed to a mountain
road with steep inclines. When we choose the path of
righteousness we tend to steer clear of steep inclines
on which we can be injured. The way of the righteous
is not cluttered with the difficult consequences of sin.
Do not be discouraged by evildoers as you walk on the
path of the righteous. God will level out the road in His
time and in His way.

# **Glorious God**

*The glory of the LORD will be revealed.*
ISAIAH 40:5

Try to imagine the glory of the Lord, and you simply can't. His glory is far greater than anything we have ever known. We have nothing on this earth to which to compare His great majesty and glory. When Moses humbly asked to see God's glory, God allowed him a glimpse of His goodness as Moses hid in the cleft of the rock and was covered by God's hand. So great is His glory that Moses' face shone with it, and he had to wear a veil when he returned to the Israelite camp.

One day we will see God's glory, and what a great and awesome day that will be! There will be no other response than to fall on our faces and worship Him. He alone is worthy of worship and adoration. Take some time alone today to bow down before Him and praise Him for His glory and majesty. He is glorious, and He will not share His glory with another.

*He Is the...*

# Everlasting God

*Do you not know? Have you not heard?*
*The LORD is the everlasting God.*
ISAIAH 40:28

God keeps on going, for He is the everlasting God, the Creator of all! It's hard for us to imagine what "everlasting" means, because everything we know from our perspective here on earth has limitations. We only observe substances that break down, grow weary, and decay, yet God lasts forever. Isaiah went on to explain, "He will not grow tired or weary, and his understanding no one can fathom."

Of all the superheroes who have ever been created, I've never seen a character who was known for their lack of fatigue. "Never Weary Man" would surely be a superhero. Only God keeps on going without slowing down. What implications does this have for us personally? We can go to Him continually, for He never slumbers or sleeps. He gives strength to us when we are weary, for He never grows weary. He never grows tired of listening to our requests.

*He...*

# Upholds Us

*I will strengthen you and help you;*
*I will uphold you with my righteous right hand.*
Isaiah 41:10

Are you worried or fearful? Are you discouraged or dismayed? God's righteous right hand is powerful and majestic and able to deliver us from our enemies, and it is with this right hand that God chooses to uphold you and me. To *uphold* means to "sustain and to help." Picture yourself safe in the palm of His loving hand. Picture Him lifting you above your circumstances and protecting you from being trampled.

God doesn't want His people to live in fear or be consumed with worry. We see this message throughout Scripture: "Do not be afraid, neither be dismayed, for the Lord your God is with you wherever you go." Knowing He is present calms our fears. Hearing His promise of strength and help keeps us from getting discouraged or dismayed.

*Father, thank You for calming my fears. You are the One who upholds me through difficulties.*

# Glory Will Not Be Shared

*I am the LORD; that is my name!*
*I will not give my glory to anyone else.*
ISAIAH 42:8 NLT

The glory of the Lord will not be shared. He alone is majestic and glorious. The word *glorious* in the original Hebrew means "splendor, wealth, great quantity, or weightiness." The glory of the Lord is to be honored and feared. It is too awesome to look upon.

In Daniel we read about King Nebuchadnezzar, who bragged about Babylon being built by his own mighty power and for the glory of his own majesty. As a result God took his honor away from him, allowing him to live like a wild animal until he acknowledged God as Most High. In Acts we read of Herod, who took the praise for himself when the people shouted that he spoke with the voice of God, not man. Immediately the angel of God struck him down because he did not give praise to God. Let us give Him and Him alone the glory due to His name.

# Makes a Way in the Desert

*Behold, I will do something new...*
*I will even make a roadway in the wilderness.*
ISAIAH 43:6 ASV

The desert is a tough place to survive, especially if you do not know where you are going. One bluff or sand dune looks like another, and you could easily go in circles if you do not have someone to guide you. We all face desert-type experiences in our lives where we may feel lost or alone, but we also must eventually get through the desert. God will make a roadway and a path in the wilderness so we don't stay there forever.

The wilderness is temporary. Do not grow comfortable there. God will make a roadway to eventually lead you to green meadows and peaceful streams. Though He does not leave you in the desert, He will teach you new truths while you are there. Allow Him to do a new work in you, and look to Him to guide you on the pathway to greener pastures.

# First and Last

*I am the first and I am the last;*
*apart from me there is no God.*

Isaiah 44:6

Israel's love for God began to fade. They became distracted and enticed by the idols of their culture. It's easy to look at the Israelites and think, *How in the world could they have done this?* Yet we must always examine our own hearts. Are there interests and desires that distract us from the One who is First and Last, our King and Redeemer? Are there people or things we have such a tight grip on that we won't let them go? Let us keep our hearts and minds bent toward the One who is First and Last.

We can go to the Redeemer, the One who always has been and always will be, and ask Him to reveal the deep-down idols of our heart.

*Father, You are the one true God. There is no other. Help us to recognize the things that distract us from You. Praise You, Father, for You are the First and the Last in my heart.*

# Does Not Forget

*Can a mother forget the baby at her breast?*
*Though she may forget, I will not forget you!*
ISAIAH 49:15

The Israelites felt as though God had forgotten them. Perhaps there have been times in your life when you felt the same way, but God does not forget His children. Although He may be silent, or it may seem that He is far off, we can be assured that He will never forget His people. Certainly a mother wouldn't forget her child, but even if she did, we know that God will not forget His children.

Do not mistake difficulties or silence as the Lord's forgetfulness, for it cannot be so. God sees. He hears. And He keeps us in the very forefront of His mind. He is attentive and involved even when we do not feel Him or see Him. Take heart in knowing that your situation has not gotten lost in an old box in the basement. He loves you and cares about the details of your life.

*His...*

# Hands Are Engraved

*See, I have engraved you on the palms of my hand.*
ISAIAH 49:16

Hundreds of years before Jesus' hands were pierced by the nails of the cross, God declared, "I have engraved you on the palms of my hands." God knew what He was going to do to demonstrate His love for us from the beginning. It was a part of His plan. The word *engraved* means indelibly imprinted or tattooed. Open up your hands right now and look at your palms. Now imagine God's hands with our pictures engraved at the very center.

Do you sense the love He has for us? What tender care—to place us in the palms of His hands! A tattoo on the palm of His hands is there every time He reaches out to touch or carry or hold. As the hand of God reaches forth to do His work, He has us in mind. We are ever before Him. What a wonderful place to be—in the palm of His hand!

*Thank You, Father, for your enduring love!*

# Man of Sorrows

*He is despised and rejected by men,*
*A Man of sorrows and acquainted with grief.*
ISAIAH 53:3 NKJV

Despised and rejected by the very creatures He created! Yes, Jesus was a Man of sorrows, and He knew grief. It is hard to imagine the heartache the Son of God must have felt as He came to bring hope and life to this dark world, and yet He was rejected. Isaiah wrote these words of the coming Messiah so that people would recognize that He was not coming as with the pomp of a prince, but rather as a Man of sorrows.

Those who know sorrow can take comfort in knowing that the Lord Himself was acquainted with sorrow and grief. He can feel the depths of our pain, for He has experienced it Himself. We can bring our sorrows to Him, knowing that He understands. He invites us to cast our cares on Him because He knows what pain is like. Bring your sorrows to the Man of sorrows, for He feels your pain.

*He Is the...*

# Perfect Husband

*For your Maker is your husband—*
*the LORD Almighty is his name.*
ISAIAH 54:5

As women it is easy for us to think that the "perfect husband" will meet all of our needs. There is only one perfect husband—the Lord Almighty. Have you ever thought of Him as your husband? He is the one who redeems us, protects us, sustains us, and cares for us. He loves us with an unfailing love and sees our deepest needs. We could ask for no better husband than Him.

He chose us to be His bride. What an amazing thought to realize that the God of all the earth wants us as His dearly beloved. Isaiah went on to say,

> I delight greatly in the LORD; my soul rejoices in my God. For he has clothed me with garments of salvation and arrayed me in a robe of his righteousness, as a bridegroom adorns his head like a priest, and as a bride adorns herself with her jewels.[63]

Rejoice, O bride, for He has made you beautiful.

# Revives the Heart

*I live in a high and holy place, but also with the one
who is contrite and lowly in spirit, to revive the spirit
of the lowly and to revive the heart of the contrite.*

ISAIAH 57:15

Perhaps you have felt unworthy, unaccepted, discouraged, or low. God is able to revive your spirit and strengthen your heart. He cares about the deepest hurts of your heart. He dwells not only in the high and holy place—He is also with those who are humble in spirit.

A lowly heart reflects one who recognizes her need for God. Often it is our brokenness that leads us back to a place of depending on Him. Jesus said, "Blessed are the poor in spirit, for theirs is the kingdom of heaven."[64] The opposite of a lowly and contrite heart is a prideful one. When we come to God with a contrite heart, repenting of our sins, He revives us and renews us. Don't let pride keep you from the renewal and refreshment He wants to bring to your life. Come humbly to Him and allow Him to revive your heart.

*He...*

# Bought Back His People

*The Redeemer will come to Jerusalem to buy back*
*those in Israel who have turned from their sins.*
ISAIAH 59:20 NLT

C an you imagine if you went to an antique store
and discovered a valuable photo album that once
belonged to your family? Somehow this precious album
had changed hands, and now it is for sale for a hefty
price. When you approach the owner to tell him it
belongs to your family, he simply shrugs his shoulders
and says, "Well, I guess if you want it you will have to
buy it back." Buy back what is rightfully yours? That
doesn't seem fair! Yet because it is of great value to you,
you give all you have in your wallet in order to redeem it.

Jesus came to buy back His precious people, and
what a price He paid. He gave His life for our redemption. He paid the debt so that all who would repent and
turn to Him would be set free.

*Thank You, Father, for buying back Your people at the*
*cost of Your Son. We live in gratitude for what You have*
*done.*

*He Is a...*

# Potter

*We are the clay, and You our potter;*
*And all we are the work of Your hand.*
ISAIAH 64:8 NKJV

A skilled potter can transform a lump of clay into a beautiful and useful vessel. In a much more magnificent way, the Lord is our Potter, molding us and making us useful vessels. He is our Creator, yet He doesn't just let us sit here on this earth like useless clumps of clay. He works with us.

A potter designs each vessel by making indentions and cuts, working the clay with his hands over and over until he forms what he has pictured in his mind all along. There is intention and purpose with each stroke. God is a patient and perfect Potter. We are in good hands as He works with us and molds us into the people He intends for us to be. Do not be discouraged by the push and pressure of His hands as He works with you. We cannot tell the Potter how to make His pottery. We must remain moldable and pliable in His hands, trusting His loving plan for us.

*He Is...*

# King of the Nations

*Who would not fear You, O King of the nations?*
*For this is Your rightful due ... There is none like You.*

JEREMIAH 10:7 NKJV

There is no king like our glorious King. Among all the rulers and wise men of every nation and kingdom, no one compares to Him. The Bible tells us that one day every nation will bow down and every tongue confess that Jesus Christ is Lord.[65] People are impressed by earthly kings, but the recognition of the greatness and holiness of the King of the nations stirs in us a healthy fear and reverence for His holiness. Some may put their trust in the United Nations, but the King of nations is the sovereign authority and ruler of the universe.

He is not only King of the nations, but also King of our hearts. We can choose to honor Him as the ruler of our hearts, or we can choose to set Him aside in a small compartment of our lives. We can use the gifts our King has given us to honor and serve Him, or we can choose to use our gifts and talents for our own gain. Worship Him as King of the nations and King of your heart.

# Turns Mourning into Gladness

*I will turn their mourning into gladness;*
*I will give them comfort and joy instead of sorrow.*

JEREMIAH 31:13

There were times when the prophet Jeremiah thought there was no possibility for redemption. God reassured Him with words of hope that speak to us today. When we cannot see the sunlight, and there is no glimmer of hope in our circumstances, all is not lost. God can turn mourning into gladness and bring comfort and even joy to replace our sorrow. He brings light and hope to the darkest pit.

Do not lose hope. Although you may not be able to imagine how joy could come from your difficulties, turn your eyes toward the God who turns mourning into gladness. Sinclair Ferguson reminds us, "The fact that we cannot see what God is doing does not mean that he is doing nothing."[66] Trust His redemptive hand, which can do far more than we can ever imagine. He brought joy from the sorrow of the cross, and He can bring joy to your sorrow as well.

# **Righteous Savior**

*This is the name by which he will be called:*
*The LORD Our Righteous Savior.*

JEREMIAH 33:16

Hundreds of years before Jesus was born, Jeremiah the prophet proclaimed that a righteous Branch would sprout from David's line, one who would be called the Lord our Righteous Savior. Jesus is the Branch whom God sent to be our Righteous Savior.

In the New Testament we read Paul's words comparing the righteousness that we have from Christ to the righteousness of our own doing. Paul said he wanted to gain Christ and be found in Him, not having a righteousness of his own that comes from the law, but that which is through faith in Christ—the righteousness that comes from God on the basis of faith.[67] We are not able to save ourselves through our own righteousness; we need a righteous savior to rescue us. Are you trying to achieve your own righteousness in God's eyes? Place your faith in your Righteous Savior—He has given you His righteousness.

*He Is Our...*

# Inheritance

*The LORD is my inheritance;*
*therefore, I will hope in him!*
LAMENTATIONS 3:24 NLT

When the prophet Jeremiah found himself at one of the lowest points in his life, there was one thought that gave him hope. He remembered that "the faithful love of the LORD never ends! His mercies never cease. Great is his faithfulness; his mercies begin afresh each morning."[68] When all else was gone, Jeremiah knew that no one could take away the Lord. God was his portion, his share, his inheritance.

An inheritance was very important to the people of Israel. As the Promised Land was apportioned to the Israelite tribes, the Levites were not given any land because the Lord was their share and their inheritance. God's mercy and faithfulness is our inheritance as well. He gives us worth and value. His love and compassion sustain us through troubled times. His faithfulness can be depended upon.

# **There**

*The name of the city from that time on will be:*
*THE LORD IS THERE.*

Ezekiel 48:35

Israel came to a point of ignoring God's holiness. The terrible result of this rebellion was that God's presence departed from the temple and from the people of Israel. Yet Ezekiel's book ends on a positive note, with his vision of the new temple and new city.

The beauty of this new city is that it will be named THE LORD IS THERE. What a glorious day when we will one day be in His presence! While we long for that day when we will be with Him in glory, let us also rejoice in His presence with us now. The Bible tells us that we are the temple of the Holy Spirit, and He is here among us and lives within us. How wonderful to think that His divine presence is with us now! May we honor His presence, recognizing Him as Holy God. Let us never be like the Israelites in Ezekiel's day, who grew lax in honoring His glory and recognizing His holiness.

*He...*

# Gives Wisdom

*He gives wisdom to the wise*
*and knowledge to the discerning.*

DANIEL 2:20-21

There is no limit to God's wisdom and understanding. In Proverbs we are reminded that wisdom was present in the creation process, and certainly we can see His wisdom as we consider all He created. In the New Testament we are reminded that in Christ all the riches of wisdom and knowledge are found.

God is our source of wisdom. The Bible tells us that the fear of the Lord is the beginning of wisdom—and that the Lord gives wisdom and from His mouth comes knowledge and understanding. Do you want to be a wise person? Begin at His feet, going to Him in humility and recognizing your need for Him. Ask Him for wisdom, because He gives generously to all who ask.

*Thank You, Lord, that we were formed in wisdom, and that You generously give wisdom to those who ask.*

*He Is the…*

# All-Knowing God

*He reveals deep and hidden things; he knows what
lies in darkness, and light dwells with him.*

**DANIEL 2:22**

God is both all-wise and all-knowing. What is the difference? Wisdom and knowledge have slightly different connotations, but both words reveal to us the infinite nature of God. Wisdom implies shrewdness and the ability to make right choices. It also can refer to special abilities and creativity. Knowledge, on the other hand, is cognitive insight and understanding. Humanly speaking, knowledge is acquired through learning, seeing, or experiencing. God does not need to learn anything, for He has always known all things. He does not need instruction, for all knowledge begins with Him.

There is nothing beyond His knowing, for He sees all and knows all. His knowledge is indefinable; it goes beyond all the books and writings ever created. Will you trust Him with the details of your life and rest in the assurance that you are in the hands of the only One who knows all things?

*He...*

# Does as He Pleases

*He does as he pleases among the angels of heaven and among the people of the earth.*

DANIEL 4:35 NLT

God alone has the right to do as He pleases. No one can stop Him. Thankfully, He is good. He is merciful as He sits on His throne with unlimited power. An earthly leader with even a small portion of power is often tempted to misuse it, and certainly throughout the ages we have seen examples of this. But not our loving and gracious Father. Although He can do whatever He wants, He does not use His power for cruel or abusive purposes.

He does what He pleases, but what He pleases is always for a good purpose because He is good. He causes even what seem like bad situations to work together for something good to those who are in Christ Jesus. In our world today, most people feel entitled to do what they please, but only God has that privilege and honor. Let us reverence Him and acknowledge Him as Lord of all.

# **Ancient of Days**

*The Ancient of Days took his seat.*
DANIEL 7:9

God is the ultimate authority. He always has been and always will be. Daniel reminds us that He alone sits in the judgment seat and will one day judge all nations. Picture the glorious vision Daniel described as he saw the Ancient of Days seated on His throne. His clothing was white as snow, and His hair white as wool. The throne was flaming with fire, and wheels were ablaze.

Daniel went on to say, "The Ancient of Days came and pronounced judgment in favor of the holy people of the Most High, and the time came when they possessed the kingdom." Because of what Christ has done on the cross, the Ancient of Days, the Most High God, will pronounce judgment in favor of those who have placed their faith in Him. Followers of Christ can look forward to the day when we will stand before His throne receiving His favor. O glorious day!

# Restores the Years

*I will restore to you the years
that the swarming locust has eaten.*

JOEL 2:25

God's people had become both prosperous and complacent. They took God for granted and turned away from following Him. The prophet Joel had a message for them, warning them of impending judgment because of their sins. He pleaded with them, saying, "Return to the LORD your God, for He *is* gracious and merciful, slow to anger, and of great kindness; And He relents from doing harm." What a beautiful message of forgiveness and hope!

Judah's land was ravaged by locusts, and Joel warned that this was only a foretaste of coming judgment. His call to repentance included the hope that all would be restored, even the years the locust had eaten. If God can restore chewed-up crops, He can restore messed-up lives. Let us hear His voice calling us to return to Him. Let us trust that when we repent, He will restore the mess we may have created by our own rebellion.

# Enables Us to Walk on High Ground

*He makes my feet like the feet of a deer,*
*he enables me to tread on the heights.*

HABAKKUK 3:19

D o not fear where the Lord is taking you, for He will equip you for the journey. He has equipped mountain deer with hooves that can scale the high mountains, and He will equip you for the heights as well. He is your strength and will give you what you need for the path. Habakkuk also reminds us that God is sovereign. He is not surprised by the heights or the valleys. He is the One in total authority. He is the One who enables you to take each step, and He is the One who gives you the ability to endure.

Rely on Him as your strength and help. Don't try to walk your road alone or tread the heights in your own strength. Turn your heart toward His loving care. If He gives the deer what they need for the high rocks and frightening cliffs, will He not equip you as well? Do not be afraid—the Sovereign Lord is your strength!

*He...*

# **Visits His People in Kindness**

*The LORD their God will visit his people in kindness.*

ZEPHANIAH 2:7

"V isitors welcome!" That's what the sign says on the door of an elderly man's room at the nursing home, yet few ever darken the door to say hello. Some are too busy, while others simply do not care. Thankfully, that is not how God treats us. He does not ignore us. He is not too busy running the universe to care about our needs. He visits His people. Because of His great kindness He does not leave us alone, but visits us and cares for our needs.

The Hebrew term for *visit* is *paqad*, meaning "to look after, to be concerned with or make a search for," and it can be used to indicate divine intervention. The word was first used in Genesis when the Lord "visited Sarah." In some cases the word *visit* is used in regard to punishment.[69] Whether for discipline or for blessing, God visits because He is kind and He cares for His people. Let us welcome this visitor in our hearts.

# **Messenger of the Covenant**

*The messenger of the covenant, whom ye desire,
behold, he cometh, saith Jehovah of hosts.*

MALACHI 3:1 ASV

John the Baptist was one of God's messengers to prepare the way for His Son. God wanted His people to be ready. In order to recognize the Messiah, their hearts needed to be prepared and ready to receive. They needed to recognize their sin so they could clearly see their need for a savior. God didn't want them to miss the Messenger of the Covenant, so He sent a messenger to prepare them ahead of time.

Jesus was the Messenger of the Covenant, and the fulfiller of God's promise. He brought a new covenant of God's grace. A messenger is one who is sent to bring information. Christ is God's ultimate messenger to this world to bring a message of hope, forgiveness, and grace. The message was simple: God loved the world so much that He sent His only Son, that whoever believes in Him will not perish but have eternal life. Now we are messengers to proclaim this good news to the world.

*He Is...*

# King of the Jews

*Magi from the east came to Jerusalem and asked,*
*"Where is the one who has been born king of the Jews?"*
MATTHEW 2:1

The Magi traveled a great distance to find the King of the Jews and worship Him. They brought gifts fitting for a king: gold, incense, and myrrh. The Bible does not tell us much about these mysterious Magi, but we do know one thing—they sought out the King, and when they found Him they were overjoyed. They bowed down and worshipped Christ, the King of the Jews. Isn't that a beautiful picture of a believer's journey? God puts in our hearts a desire for Him. We seek Him, and when we find Him we are filled with joy, for at last we have found the only King who can satisfy our souls.

What gifts do you bring to the King of the Jews? It seems so often we are seeking what we can get, not what we can give; yet we all have gifts to give Him. As we love and serve others, even the least of these we are serving Him. Honor the King with your words of thanksgiving and deeds of service.

# Separates the Chaff from the Wheat

*He is ready to separate the chaff from the wheat
with his winnowing fork.*
MATTHEW 3:12 NLT

The winnowing fork looked something like a pitchfork. It was used to toss the grain in the air in order to separate the kernels of wheat from the chaff. The worthless outer shell of the kernel (the chaff) was destroyed, while the wheat went to useful purposes. The winnowing fork is used as a picture of judgment. This passage goes on to say, "Then he will clean up the threshing area, gathering the wheat into his barn but burning the chaff with never-ending fire."

The Bible is clear that there will be a judgment one day. Those who are repentant and place their faith in God are the wheat, while those who choose to go their own way will be cast into never-ending fire. Without Christ, our lives are like useless chaff in this world, blown about by the winds of the culture. With Christ we have meaning and purpose and hope. Are you wheat or are you chaff? Christ makes the difference.

*He Is...*

# **Perfect!**

*Be perfect, therefore,*
*as your heavenly Father is perfect.*

MATTHEW 5:48

Perfect is an overused word in our vocabulary today. *What a perfect little baby! She's the perfect candidate for the job. He's the perfect man for her!* If we are going to be perfectly honest, there is no one who is perfect except God Himself. The word *perfect* actually means "complete or lacking nothing." God is complete; there is nothing He needs, and nothing can be added to Him.

We, on the other hand, need some work. We certainly are not perfect. Yet why would Jesus tell us to be perfect if we can't be perfect? Certainly we can aspire to live a righteous life, but we will always fall short. The only way we can be complete or perfect is in Christ. He completes us. The One who is perfect gave His life so that we may be made perfect and complete in Him.

# Rewards Us

*When you pray, go into your room, close the door and*
*pray to your Father, who is unseen. Then your Father,*
*who sees what is done in secret, will reward you.*

MATTHEW 6:6

God wants us to spend time alone in private prayer. There may be times when we pray together with others, but that shouldn't be the only time we pray. God doesn't want us to neglect a private time of prayer with Him alone. Our Father who is unseen knows what happens in the secret places. He rewards those who seek Him.

He rewards us for the things done in secret, not for show. Throughout Scripture we read about the rewards He offers. In James we read, "Blessed is the one who perseveres under trial because, having stood the test, that person will receive the crown of life that the Lord has promised to those who love him." God rewards His faithful ones. The greatest reward of all will be to live with Him in glory. Let us enjoy the reward of abiding in Him here on earth and look forward to the day when we will see Him face-to-face.

*He...*

# Sees What Is Done in Secret

*Your Father, who is unseen ... sees what is done in secret.*

MATTHEW 6:18

God knows what happens in private. We cannot hide from Him. When we feel alone or unjustly treated, there is comfort in knowing that He sees all. Nothing is hidden or kept secret from Him. This is not only comforting, but also convicting. How silly it is to think that we can hide something from God. In the Garden of Eden, Adam and Eve thought they could hide their sin from Him. Yet from the first sin until now, God sees what is done in secret.

Video surveillance is often used today to help prevent robberies or crimes. Why? Because when people know they are being watched or can be identified, they clean up their act. Signs are posted to remind would-be robbers that they are being observed. God's Word acts as a sign to remind us that we are being watched. God, who is unseen, sees what is done in secret.

*He Is the...*

# Beloved

*This is My beloved Son. Hear Him!*

**MARK 9:7 NKJV**

H oly and dearly loved. Jesus is God's only Son and the object of His love. Yet God in His amazing grace toward us allowed Him to become the sacrifice for our sins. Oh, how much the Father must love us to have sent His Beloved One on our behalf! The word *beloved* in Greek is *agapetos*. Do you recognize the word *agape* in it? *Agape* love is the highest form of love. It is the deep, self-sacrificing, and pure love of God.

Jesus is not only God's Beloved One, but He is *our* Beloved One as well, for He laid down His life on our behalf. Paul reminds us, "He has rescued us from the dominion of darkness and brought us into the kingdom of the Son he loves."[70] As a Prince Charming saves his princess, so our Beloved One has saved us, in order that we too may be holy and, as sons and daughters, dearly loved by the Father.

# Son of God

*The holy one to be born will be called the Son of God.*

LUKE 1:35

Mary, blessed among women, was the one chosen to bear God's Son here on earth. Isaiah prophesied that a virgin would bear a son, and hundreds of years later, the virgin Mary received the glorious news that the Son of God was to be born of her. The title *Son of God* carried great significance. As God's Son, He was the long-awaited Messiah. Jesus called Himself "God's only begotten Son."

It was the very title *Son of God* that led Jesus' enemies to crucify Him for claiming to be God. We read in the Gospel of John, "The Jewish leaders insisted, 'According to that law he [Jesus] must die, because he claimed to be the Son of God.'"[71] They did not crucify Jesus for healing on the Sabbath or teaching about the kingdom of heaven. They killed Him because He claimed to be the very Son of God. The power of that name brings with it the claim of being one with God, just as Jesus had said: "I and my Father are One."

*He Is the...*

# **Savior**

*A Savior has been born to you.*
LUKE 2:11

The angel proclaimed the most important and powerful message this world could ever imagine: "A Savior has been born to you." Mankind needed rescuing. Although some were looking for a political savior to rescue the Israelites from the heavy hand of Rome, Jesus came as a different kind of savior. The scope of His rescue reached far beyond the dominance of Rome. He came to save us from the domination of sin.

Christ saved us from eternal punishment. He is the Savior to all who believe. Sadly, many people don't think they need a savior. They scoff at the phrase "Jesus saves," wondering what they need to be saved from. We must recognize our own personal sin before we know that we need a savior. The Bible says that all have sinned and fallen short of His glory. It also says that the wages of sin is death, but the gift of God is eternal life through Jesus Christ our Lord. Is He your Savior?

*He Is the...*

# Glory of Israel

*He is a light to reveal God to the nations,*
*and he is the glory of your people Israel!*
LUKE 2:30-32 NLT

When Simeon, a devout Israelite awaiting God's Messiah, saw the baby Jesus he took Him in his arms and praised God. In our passage today we see Simeon's proclamation of who Jesus is and why He came. He is a light to reveal God to the nations, and He is the glory of Israel. Known as the Canticle of Simeon, or the Nunc Dimittis, it is still sung in evening prayers in Orthodox churches, representing the confession and experience of believers.

The Savior of the world came through the Jewish nation. Jesus was the crowning glory of God's people Israel, although they did not recognize or honor Him. The Israelites were the chosen people from whom the Light of all nations would come. What a privileged and honored people they are! Jesus, the light to reveal God to the nations, came through them.

# Joyful

*You are my dearly loved Son,*
*and you bring me great joy.*
LUKE 3:22 NLT

Do you ever think of God as joyful? I know we recognize Him as holy, majestic, loving, and powerful...but joyful? Yet the Bible tells us that one of the fruits of His Spirit is joy. We are reminded in Psalms that He delights in the details of our lives. Zephaniah prophesied that God would take delight in His people with gladness and rejoice over them with joyful songs. Nehemiah encouraged God's people by telling them, "The joy of the LORD is your strength."

Yes, God is a God of joy, and He encourages us to be joyful too. Throughout Scripture we are reminded to rejoice in the Lord. As we turn our eyes toward our joyful Father and recognize His love, care, and provision, we too can rejoice! We may not find our joy in circumstances or in people, but we can find our joy in the Lord. Rejoice in the God of joy!

# Kind

*He is kind to the ungrateful and wicked.*
LUKE 6:35

God is not kind only to those who are pleasant, nice, and good. We see in our passage today that He is kind to the ungrateful and wicked as well. In His infinite power He could annihilate anyone He wants to, especially His enemies, yet He shows continual mercy and grace. We are recipients of His kindness every day. In the same way, Jesus told His followers to love their enemies, do good to them, and lend to them without expecting anything in return. God is kind even to His enemies.

Kindness is a fruit of God's spirit. We can go to Him who overflows with kindness and ask for His help in being kind to others. Just think what this world would look like if we treated everyone we met with a God-like kindness. Take time each day to thank Him for His kindness toward you and then ask Him to help you extend His kindness toward others.

# **Suffering Servant**

*The Son of Man must suffer many things.*
LUKE 9:22

Jesus predicted His own suffering. When He came to this earth He knew He was not coming to be comfortable and enjoy a good time. He came knowing He would suffer many things and be rejected. He knew He must not only suffer, but die on our behalf. As followers of Christ we too may face challenges, obstacles, persecution, and even suffering, just as our Lord did. Do not be surprised if you suffer for His sake, but rather remember that He too suffered on our behalf.

The apostle Paul said, "I want to know Christ—yes, to know the power of his resurrection and participation in his sufferings, becoming like him in his death, and so, somehow, attaining to the resurrection from the dead."[72] We may experience some suffering in this life, but we will also experience His resurrection as well. One day we will be with Him in glory and suffer no more.

*He...*

# Runs to Us

*His father saw him and was filled with
compassion for him; he ran to his son, threw
his arms around him and kissed him.*

LUKE 15:20

The Father's love is so beautifully portrayed in the parable of the Prodigal Son. The son demanded his inheritance from his father early, which was considered a terrible affront. He went off and squandered his wealth until he had nothing left. When he was at his lowest point, wanting to eat food scraps in the mud with the pigs, he remembered his father's kind heart. He realized that even his father's servants lived better than this, so he began the humble journey home.

Picture the beauty of this father, filled with compassion, running toward his son. He didn't have to do it! Yet he ran to his son, threw his arms around him, and kissed him. I can't help but think of Psalm 23: "Surely your goodness and unfailing love will pursue me all the days of my life." Our Father runs to us with arms open wide, filled with love and compassion.

*He...*

# Knows Our Hearts

*God knows your hearts. What people value
highly is detestable in God's sight.*

LUKE 16:15

What we tend to value outwardly in people, God may find detestable. This was the case with the Pharisees, who appeared so perfectly religious, and yet their hearts were filthy and ugly. God knows what is in our hearts. We need to be more concerned about our inward appearance than our outward one. It's easy to look good by doing all sorts of religious things or church activities, but what is our motive? Are we doing these things out of love for God? Or out of love for ourselves, and so people will think we are great?

It's hard to know our hearts and nearly impossible to have completely pure motives, but we can ask God to create in us a clean heart. Don't go around judging other people's motives, for only He knows the heart. Be diligent to guard your own heart and live wholeheartedly for Him.

*He Is the...*

# Word

*In the beginning was the Word, and the Word
was with God, and the Word was God.*

John 1:1

In John's day "the Word" was a significant term to both philosophers and theologians. In the Hebrew Scriptures the Word was not only the means God used to create the world, but also the way He spoke through the prophets and gave His law to His people. To the Hebrew teachers, the Word represented God. For the Greek philosophers, the Word was the principle of reason, which governed society. When John identified Jesus as the Word, he was declaring Him to be God and the governing authority.

Words are powerful. They can set entire nations at odds. They can bring peace to a home or a business or they can create great hostility within a family or company. Words leave an indelible mark. How has the Word affected your life?

### *He Is the...*

# Lamb of God

*Look, the Lamb of God, who takes*
*away the sin of the world!*

JOHN 1:29

In the Old Testament, a lamb without blemish was slain in payment for the sins of God's people. In our passage today, John the Baptist proclaims Jesus as the Lamb who takes away the sin of the world. He was identifying what Jesus had come to this earth to do. Many of the Jews were looking for a Messiah who would deliver them from Roman rule, but Jesus was the Messiah who came to lay down His life to deliver His followers from the penalty of sin.

Hundreds of years earlier the prophet Isaiah talked about the Messiah, saying, "We all, like sheep, have gone astray, each of us has turned to our own way; and the LORD has laid on Him the iniquity of us all." O Beautiful Lamb! Because of His sacrifice, we are healed from the scars of our sin.

*Thank You, Father, for sending the Lamb of God, Your beloved Son on our behalf. We did not deserve Your kindness, but because of the Lamb we live our lives in thanks to You.*

*He Is the...*

# Chosen One

*I have seen and I testify that this is God's Chosen One.*
JOHN 1:34

John the Baptist knew what his purpose was in life. He was to prepare the way for the Messiah and point people to Him. When John baptized Jesus he saw the Spirit come down from heaven as a dove and remain on Jesus. John then proclaimed, "I have seen and I testify that this is God's Chosen One." Jesus the Chosen One. We know that Jesus was God's Chosen One to bear the punishment for our sin.

John's use of the term *Chosen One* holds great strength, as the title points to the One for whom the world had been waiting. *Chosen One* identifies Jesus as unique and in a class all His own. He wasn't one of many, He was *the* Chosen One. In a world that was searching for someone to follow, John pointed everyone to Jesus. We too can be like John, identifying and pointing others toward the Chosen One.

*Father, let my light shine for You and point people to You in this dark world.*

*He Is the...*

# Messiah

*"We have found the Messiah" (that is,
the Christ). And he brought him to Jesus.*

JOHN 1:41

The title *Messiah* is a Hebrew word, translated into Greek as *Christ*. They both mean "Anointed One," representing the one whom God especially appointed for His plan and purpose. Jesus is that Anointed One. He is the long-awaited Messiah. When Andrew met Jesus, the first thing he did was run to tell his brother, Simon. He couldn't contain his excitement, for he had discovered the One who was a life-changer, the One and Only, the Anointed One of God.

Andrew brought his brother to Jesus because he was excited, thrilled, and overcome with joy. His heart was prepared—he had eagerly awaited the Messiah's arrival. He couldn't hide his enthusiasm. Interestingly the word *enthusiasm* means "God within." We can't help but be enthusiastic when we meet Christ and have God within our hearts. Who is the Messiah to you? Is He just a nice man, or is He a life-changer? Embrace Him enthusiastically!

*He Is the…*

# Stairway Between Heaven and Earth

*You will all see heaven open and the angels of God
going up and down on the Son of Man, the one
who is the stairway between heaven and earth.*

JOHN 1:51 NLT

Jesus introduced Himself to Nathanael by referring to a story in Genesis. The Old Testament patriarch Jacob had a dream of a stairway that reached from earth to heaven. In the dream God promised that all families of the earth would be blessed through him and his descendants.[73]

Now the stairway had come, the one who bridges the gap between heaven and earth. There is only one stairway to heaven, and it is Christ. Jesus used this unique way to describe Himself to Nathanael most likely because he was a devoted Jew waiting for the promise of God to be fulfilled. Jesus knew the term "stairway to heaven" would speak directly to Nathanael's Jewish upbringing and knowledge of God's law. Jesus knows exactly what speaks to our hearts and minds.

*Father, thank You for knowing our hearts and drawing us to Yourself.*

*He Performs...*
# **Miraculous Signs**

*Because of the miraculous signs Jesus did in Jerusalem at
the Passover celebration, many began to trust in him.*

JOHN 2:23 NLT

People needed reassurance that Jesus wasn't just a man or a prophet, but the Son of God. Jesus performed miracle upon miracle. He changed water into wine, fed the 5000, healed the sick, gave sight to the blind, made the lame walk, and even raised Lazarus from the dead. Many began to trust, yet others had hardened hearts and refused to follow Him.

C.S. Lewis said, "The miracles in fact are a retelling in small letters of the very same story which is written across the whole world in letters too large for some of us to see."[74] Some see it and some don't, but God is in the miracle business. We see His miraculous work in His creation, we see it in the miracles Jesus performed, and we see it in the transforming work He does in each of our lives.

*He...*

# Knows Human Nature

*Jesus didn't trust them, because he knew human nature.*
JOHN 2:24 NLT

No one needed to tell Jesus what people were really like. He knew because He was there at creation, and He sees inside every heart. Jesus knew that He couldn't trust people. Mankind's sinfulness didn't come as a surprise to Him. What is surprising is the fact that Jesus died on behalf of sinful men and women like us.

In Romans we read, "Very rarely will anyone die for a righteous person, though for a good person someone might possibly dare to die. But God demonstrates his own love for us in this: While we were still sinners, Christ died for us."[75] Certainly, Jesus demonstrated a great love for us to die for us knowing our sinful hearts. "Amazing love! How can it be, that Thou, my God, shouldst die for me?"

*He...*

# Gives Birth to Spiritual Life

*Flesh gives birth to flesh,*
*but the Spirit gives birth to spirit.*

JOHN 3:6

When Nicodemus, a respected religious leader, approached Jesus at night, Jesus told him no one can see the kingdom of God unless he is born again. Born again? How can that happen? Can we be born from our mother's womb again? Jesus distinguished between physical birth and spiritual birth. Flesh gives birth to flesh in physical birth, but when we are born again spiritually, God's Spirit gives birth to our spirit.

This is a mystery, and yet so very beautiful. The Bible says that before we knew Christ we were dead spiritually, but God made us alive in Him.[76] God's Spirit gives birth to our spiritual life. Just as a baby doesn't create himself or give birth to himself, so we cannot give spiritual life to ourselves. It is God's Spirit who gives birth to us.

*Thank You, Father, for the spiritual birth we experience through Your Holy Spirit. Continue to do a transforming work in our lives.*

# Lifted Up

*As Moses lifted up the bronze snake on a pole in the
wilderness, so the Son of Man must be lifted up, so that
everyone who believes in him will have eternal life.*

JOHN 3:14-15

In the Old Testament we read the story of God's
punishment of the Israelites in the wilderness. They
spoke against Moses and against God, so He sent poisonous snakes. When the people cried out and repented,
God gave them a way to be healed from the poisonous bites of the snakes. He instructed Moses to make a
bronze snake and put it on a pole. Anyone who looked
to the snake on the pole would live.[77]

Look and live. What a beautiful illustration of the
gospel of Christ! Sin has poisoned our lives, but Jesus
became sin for us when He was lifted up on the cross.
We look to the cross and our sin is forgiven. By His
stripes we are healed from the poison of our sin. Look
and live. So simple, yet so powerful. It is the cross of
Christ that saves us. He was lifted up on our behalf.
Look to Him and live.

*He...*

# Loves the World

*God so loved the world that he gave his one
and only Son, that whoever believes in him
shall not perish but have eternal life.*

JOHN 3:16

God loves the world. Ponder the depth of that one simple statement. Although we have turned from Him and gone our own way, He still loved us. All of us. Not just the righteous ones, not just the ones that go to church, not just the ones born in America. He loved the world, the people He created. And because He loves the world, He wanted to provide a way of salvation for all people. He didn't make it difficult for them—in fact He did all the work on the cross.

The Bible reminds us that those who have the Son have life, but those who do not have the Son do not have life. He provided a way for all to come to Him through Jesus. In a world filled with hatred, we have a message of love from the God of love. Let us faithfully share His message of love and hope to a hurting world.

*Father, put someone in our path today who needs to know of Your love. Help us to share Your message clearly.*

# **Sent to Save**

*God did not send his Son into the world to condemn*
*the world, but to save the world through him.*

JOHN 3:17

Jesus was not sent to this world to condemn it or judge it. He came for one purpose: to save it. Although He showed us a wonderful example of love and forgiveness, He did not come just to show the world an example of pure goodness. He came to save it. Although He healed many people while He was here on this earth, He did not come to heal the world physically. He came to heal the world spiritually by saving our souls.

Wisdom poured from His mouth as He taught about how to live in this world and about the kingdom of God, but Jesus didn't just come to teach us. He came specifically to save us. God knew we couldn't save ourselves—that's why He sent Christ. Those who wonder how a good God could send people to eternal condemnation have missed the point of why Jesus came. God sent Jesus so that the world would be saved. "Believe in the Lord Jesus, and you will be saved."[78]

## *He Gives...*
# Living Water

*Jesus replied, "If you only knew the gift God
has for you and who I am, you would ask
me, and I would give you living water."*
JOHN 4:10 NLT

Have you ever eaten something salty, and then for the next few hours you can't get enough water? Figuratively speaking, there are many salty things in this world—many interests and desires that make us thirsty for acceptance and fulfillment. We try to satisfy the thirst in a variety of unsatisfying ways, through people or things or addictions. There is only one who can quench the thirst this salty world creates, and that is Christ alone. He is the Living Water. When we look to Him to quench our desire, we thirst no more.

The woman at the well tried to find fulfillment in husband after husband. Jesus knew her deepest needs and told her, "Those who drink the water I give will never be thirsty again. It becomes a fresh, bubbling spring within them, giving them eternal life." Oh the joy and satisfaction Jesus brings to our thirsty hearts! Take your thirsts to Him.

*He Is...*

# Spirit

*God is Spirit, so those who worship him
must worship in spirit and in truth.*

JOHN 4:24 NLT

Unlike the bronze idols, the one true living God is Spirit. He is not some man-made, manufactured object. A spirit is beyond the physical realm of this world. It does not submit to the laws of gravity or physics and can come and go as it pleases. It cannot be confined or boxed in, held down or locked up. God goes far beyond what we can sense, see, taste, touch, or smell, yet like we can see the wind's effects, we can feel His presence and see His work.

God, who is Spirit, must be worshipped in spirit and in truth. What does Jesus mean by the phrase "in spirit and in truth"? God has given His Spirit to us as believers to dwell within us. In the Old Testament, God's presence could be entered only by the high priest going into the Holy of Holies in the tabernacle or temple. Now we can go to God directly, our spirit to His. We are able to worship God in spirit and in truth because of what Jesus did for us.

# Carries Out the Father's Will

*I carry out the will of the one who
sent me, not my own will.*

JOHN 5:30 NLT

Jesus and the Father were one. He did not do anything separate from His Father. Both their judgment and their will coordinated perfectly. Jesus only carried out the Father's will, not demanding His own way or His own rights. Our passage today shows us that He would not and could not do anything of His own accord. How beautifully they work together! Like a hand in a glove, so they fit perfectly together and worked in coordination with one another.

All the way to the cross, Jesus said, "Not as I will, but as you will." Through temptation and torture, He continued to willingly give up His right to go His own way in order to follow His Father's will. Let us follow our Savior, submitting our will to His. May we be able to say, as Jesus did, that we carried out the will of Him who created us.

# Multiplies Our Gifts

*Jesus then took the loaves, gave thanks, and distributed to those who were seated as much as they wanted. He did the same with the fish.*

JOHN 6:11

With more than 5000 mouths to feed, the disciples couldn't imagine how there would be enough. Philip reasoned that eight months' worth of wages wouldn't be enough to feed the people. Andrew found a boy with five loaves of bread and two fish, but wasn't sure how that would help. Jesus took what little there was and multiplied it to the point that there were 12 baskets of leftovers.

God is able to take what little we have to offer and use it in great and mighty ways. What seems small and insignificant to us can be used by God to bless many people. What do you have to offer? It may be as simple as a listening ear, a praying heart, or an open home. Bring your gifts and talents, no matter how small they may seem to you, and put them in Jesus' hands. He is able to take even the smallest gifts and use them to feed many hungry souls.

# Defies the Laws of Nature

*They saw Jesus approaching the
boat, walking on the water.*

JOHN 6:18-19

The laws of nature apply to us, but not to God. When Jesus walked on the water He demonstrated His unique ability to act and live beyond the constraints of what we experience in this world. The disciples were frightened when they saw Him walking toward their boat. They probably thought He was a ghost, but Jesus reassured them, telling them not to be afraid. After all the miracles they had seen Him do, you would think they would learn to expect the unexpected.

He does work in unexpected ways sometimes. When the storms of life begin to make your life rough, remember that the Jesus who walked on water is able to do the unexpected in your life. Do not be afraid. Place your trust in the God who loves you and walks into your situation in unexpected ways.

# Seal of Approval

*On him [Jesus] God the Father has
placed his seal of approval.*

JOHN 6:27

When it comes to manufactured products, a seal of approval is a coveted honor. It indicates to the buyer that this product is dependable and will do what it is designed to do. Although a seal of approval on a product may be a good recommendation, nothing is better than having the seal of approval from God. The Greek word *spragizo* used here indicates a stamp of authentication by God. Kings and wealthy merchants used their signet rings or private marks as a stamp for security and preservation.

Jesus was stamped with God's mark of approval. This is a guarantee we can depend upon. When we buy a product we are trusting the stamp of approval. When we place our faith in Christ and choose to invest our life in Him, we can be assured that we are placing our lives in someone worth living for. We can confidently and wholeheartedly dedicate our lives to the One who has God's seal of approval.

*He...*

# **Wants Us to Believe**

*This is the only work God wants from
you: Believe in the one he has sent.*

JOHN 6:29 NLT

The crowds said to Jesus, "We want to perform God's works too. What should we do?"[79] People tend to ask the same question today. We want to perform for God to get His seal of approval, but He requires just one thing. Jesus made it clear that the work God wants from us is to believe in the One He has sent, Jesus. This is actually a hard saying, because deep down inside our guilt makes us want to perform and do something to earn God's approval. God has evened out the playing field. He has made a way for all to please Him, through faith.

In Hebrews we are reminded that without faith it is impossible to please Him.[80] Many religions in our world today are based on performing for a deity or deities. Even Christian groups and people try to send the message that belief is not enough. Certainly our belief is evidenced by our actions, but let us heed today's passage closely: The work God wants us to do is to believe in Jesus.

# Draws Us to Himself

*No one can come to me unless the Father*
*who sent me draws them to me.*

JOHN 6:44

Although you may think someone's salvation is in your hands, it is not. In pride we may be tempted to think that we drew someone to the Lord, but it is God who draws people to Himself. Certainly He uses us in the process, but it is He who moves in someone's heart and brings them to faith. He reveals Himself to those who will come. The power for salvation is in His hands, not ours.

We must be faithful to share the wonderful salvation message and the forgiveness we have in Christ, but we must leave the results to God. We cannot force anyone to follow Christ and believe in Him. Faith is a heart issue. It must come from within. So let us be faithful to pray to the Father, who draws people to Himself. Let us not grow weary in sharing His truth, but may we always remember that the final result is in His hands.

## *He Is the...*
# Bread of Life

*I am the living bread that came down from
heaven. Whoever eats this bread will live forever.*

John 6:51

The Israelites received bread (manna) from heaven as they journeyed in the wilderness, but here we read Jesus' declaration that He is the bread of life, the bread that came down from heaven. After the Israelites ate the manna, they still became hungry the next day, but Jesus offered His life so we would hunger no more. In Him we are spiritually satisfied; we need no other. Jesus said, "I am the bread of life. Whoever comes to me will never go hungry, and whoever believes in me will never be thirsty."[81]

What did Jesus mean by eating this bread? It means inviting Him into our lives and devoting our lives to Him. Jesus isn't just someone we know about in our minds—He is someone who lives in our lives, who affects our very being. As we take the Lord's Supper we reflect on the fact that the Bread of Life was broken for us. As we eat the bread we are reminded of the Bread of Life giving His life for us. Take and eat.

# Gives Eternal Life

*The Spirit alone gives eternal life.*
*Human effort accomplishes nothing.*
JOHN 6:63 NLT

Have you ever had one of those dreams where you are running and running and getting nowhere? All the effort you are exerting is for nothing, like a gerbil running inside a wheel. Jesus made a bold statement to the Pharisees who loved to perform in front of others by keeping all the rules. They believed all their efforts gave them greater standing with both God and man, but really they were just like gerbils running inside a wheel. Jesus said their human effort accomplished nothing toward eternal life.

We can see how this announcement must have angered and frustrated them, because they had built their whole life on meticulously following the rules. Jesus' message was clear—it is not man's effort reaching up to heaven, but God's work reaching down to earth that gives us eternal life. His Spirit gives us life. It is a gift from Him—all we do is receive it.

*Thank You, Father, that You provide the way to eternal life.*

*He...*

# Speaks Like No One Else

*"No one ever spoke the way this man
does," the guards replied.*

JOHN 7:46

Jesus caused quite a stir among the crowds. Some believed He was the Messiah, while others questioned His heritage and background. The Pharisees were skeptical and jealous of Jesus, so they sent the temple guards to arrest Him. This simple assignment shouldn't have posed a problem for the guards, who were accustomed to arresting people all the time. It wasn't hard to find Jesus, since He was surrounded by crowds listening to His words.

The guards came back empty-handed. They had disobeyed orders. Why? They couldn't get over how Jesus spoke and what He had to say. He spoke with authority and wisdom, for He spoke the very words of God. The guards met the unexpected. They knew immediately that this was not an ordinary man. Jesus' words had a surprising and dramatic effect on the guards. How do Jesus' words affect your life?

## He Is the...
# Light of the World

*I am the light of the world. Whoever follows me will
never walk in darkness, but will have the light of life.*

JOHN 8:12

Jesus, the light of the world. Without Him this world would be a dark place. His light brings joy, forgiveness, love, and hope to our lives. He says as we follow Him we will not walk in darkness, but in the light of life. A heart without Jesus would be a place of despair, unforgiveness, hatred, fear, and guilt. Yet when His light shines into the heart of someone who follows Him, the light of His love overcomes the darkness.

Jesus is the light of life, and He has given us light to shine brightly into all the world. What about the darkness around you? Does the light of Jesus shine brightly through you dispelling the darkness? Be bold, be bright. Do not hide His light. Radiate His love and forgiveness to warm up and light up a cold, dark place.

*Father, thank You for being the light in my darkness. Shine brightly through me, so all the world may know Your redeeming love.*

*He...*

# Does Not Belong to This World

*Jesus continued … "You belong to this world; I do not."*
JOHN 8:23 NLT

Jesus lived in this world, but He was not *of* this world.
He came from the heavenly Father. He was all man
and all God. Jesus was unlike anyone in this world
because His heritage and lineage was from God as well
as from David. In our verse today we find Jesus carrying on a discussion with the Pharisees. He went on to
tell them, "Unless you believe that I AM who I claim to
be, you will die in your sins."

We have a choice. We can either believe that Jesus
is who He claimed to be, the Son of God, or we can die
in our sins. Sadly, many of the Pharisees chose not to
believe. Those who choose to believe in Christ become
citizens of heaven. Like Jesus, we live in this world but
we don't belong to it any longer. We have a new citizenship, and we eagerly await the day we will be with Him
and see Him face-to-face.

# **Before Abraham**

*I tell you the truth, before Abraham was even born, I AM!*
JOHN 8:58

Jesus made many bold statements throughout His ministry here on earth, but this one in particular evoked immediate anger from the Pharisees. The Bible tells us that when Jesus said, "Before Abraham was even born, I AM," the Pharisees picked up stones to stone Him. Why did this one statement cause such intense anger to erupt among the Pharisees? In saying He existed before Abraham, Jesus was saying He existed before the Israelite people existed. He used God's holy name, "I AM," identifying Himself as one with the Father. This was one of the most powerful statements Jesus ever made.

To the Pharisees, Jesus' statement was blasphemy because they closed their eyes and ears to the truth. They were so distracted by the rules of God's law that they missed the message of God's Messiah. In no uncertain terms Jesus claimed to be God. We can ignore it or we can passionately pursue Him.

*He...*

# Goes Ahead of Us

*He goes on ahead of them, and his sheep*
*follow him because they know his voice.*

JOHN 10:4

As our Good Shepherd, Jesus walks ahead of us, leading us and guiding us. In regard to salvation, He went before us, paying the penalty for our sin and rising again to give us the promise of eternal life. He went before us to heaven to prepare a place for us. He continually goes before us day by day, leading us down the right path. David put it this way, "He guides me down the right paths bringing honor to His name."[82]

We can walk in confidence as we follow our Shepherd's leading. We are His sheep, and we recognize His voice. We heard it when He called us to follow Him, and we hear it as He leads us along life's paths. We come to recognize His voice as we study and know His Word. Let us keep our eyes on the Shepherd and our ears attuned to His voice as He goes ahead of us, leading us and guiding us.

# The Gate

*I am the gate; whoever enters through me will be saved.*
JOHN 10:9

In Jesus' day, a good shepherd would lead his flock into a pen at night and then would lie down at the opening to protect his sheep from the wolves or from other predators. The shepherds used caves, sheds, or even open areas surrounded with makeshift walls of branches and rocks. The shepherd served as the literal gate for the pen, letting the sheep in and out of their place of protection.

As our gate, Jesus is our Protector, our Shepherd, and our Savior. Through Him we have access to the Father. Those who go through Him will be saved. Just as sheep "come in and go out and find pasture," so Jesus invites us to abide with Him, live with Him, dwell with Him. As the gate, the Shepherd laid down his life for His sheep. Oh what love our Shepherd has for us!

*He...*

# Came to Give Us Abundant Life

*I have come that they may have life, and have it to the full.*
JOHN 10:10

The thief comes to steal, kill, and destroy, yet Jesus came that we might have life and have it to the fullest measure! The word for "full" is the Greek word *perissos*, which means "superabundant, beyond measure, excessive." Jesus wanted us to enjoy the fullness of life to the greatest extent. He wasn't a killjoy—He was a have-joy! Truly we experience a rich and full life when we walk in fellowship with Him.

To experience abundant life means to be richly fulfilled, not by monetary wealth, but by the meaningful wealth of purpose, love, joy, and peace. God enriches our life with purpose. He loves us with a true love that flows from the wellspring of our hearts and pours out to others. When our eyes are on Him we experience a lasting joy that rises above our circumstances and an eternal peace in knowing He cares for our needs. Yes, life is full and abundant each day in Him!

*He Is the...*

# Good Shepherd

*I am the good shepherd; I know my
sheep and my sheep know me.*

John 10:14-15

Jesus is the Good Shepherd. We can trust His goodness as He cares for us, His beloved sheep. He knows us and looks out for our well-being. Sadly, sheep often stray and foolishly go their own way. The good shepherd pursues them and brings them back into the safety of the fold. He will not give up on us. He knows us by name. Isn't it a wonderful thought to know that Jesus knows us personally? We are not some number in a multitude of people—we are His, and He knows us.

In Jesus' day, when shepherds brought their flocks together in one large area, the shepherd would simply call out to his sheep, and they would recognize his voice. They followed the voice they knew and loved. Such a beautiful relationship between shepherd and sheep! The Good Shepherd knows us and cares for us. We listen for His voice and follow Him.

*He Is the...*

# **Resurrection and the Life**

*Jesus said unto her, I am the resurrection, and the life:
he that believeth on me, though he die, yet shall he live.*
JOHN 11:25 ASV

Only God has the power to resurrect someone. He raised Lazarus from the dead. He Himself rose from the dead, and He will resurrect us from the dead as well. He alone has power over death. With Jesus' resurrection came the hope and promise that as believers we too will have victory over death and live with Him in eternity. What a wonderful joy and reassurance to know that because Jesus is the Resurrection, we too will be resurrected one day.

Jesus also said He is the Life. He created life, He is the sustainer of life, and He offers eternal life. In Him we have abundant life here on earth and a joyful anticipation of life with Him. Life is meaningless and purposeless and hopeless without Him. He is our Life. When our lives seem overwhelming or frustrating, we can look to the One who is Life for renewal and strength.

# Prepares a Place for Us

*I go to prepare a place for you.*

JOHN 14:2 NKJV

Our home here on this earth is simply temporary. We have a much better place to look forward to. Jesus told His disciples, "In My Father's house are many mansions…I go to prepare a place for you. And if I go and prepare a place for you, I will come again and receive you to Myself; that where I am, *there* you may be also." How wonderful to think that Jesus is preparing a place for us in the Father's wonderful and glorious house! If He is preparing it then we know it will be a beautiful place.

Are you preparing for that home, or are you consumed with this one? It's easy to allow our lives to be consumed with the here and now, thinking that this is all there is, but we have something so much better to look forward to. Let us be diligent about laying up treasures there. One day our Lord will come back for us to take us to that wonderful heavenly kingdom. Let us live with our hearts and minds set on that place!

# The Way

*Jesus answered, "I am the way and the truth and the life. No one comes to the Father except through me."*

JOHN 14:6

Jesus is the route, the path, the road to God. He didn't leave room for any confusion. He said that no one comes to God except through Him. In other words, there are no other ways or paths. He is *the* Way. One must walk down the road of Christ to come to the Father. It's interesting that when the Jewish leaders tried to test Jesus, they came to Him saying, "Teacher, we know that you are a man of integrity and that you teach the way of God in accordance with the truth. You aren't swayed by others, because you pay no attention to who they are."[83] They recognized that Jesus taught the way of God in accordance with the truth. Sadly, they did not acknowledge Him as the Way to God and the Truth.

Do you see Jesus as the Way or just a good man talking about a way? Is He just a man who speaks in accordance with the truth, or do you recognize that He embodies truth because He is truth? He is the way, the truth, and the life.

# Perfect Teacher

*The Advocate, the Holy Spirit, whom the Father*
*will send in my name, will teach you all things and*
*will remind you of everything I have said to you.*

JOHN 14:26

We have all had a not-so-perfect teacher at some point in our education, but there is one perfect teacher—the Holy Spirit. The word translated "advocate" actually means helper, counselor, or comforter. It's one who comes to your side or your aid when you need him. Isn't that a picture of a perfect teacher? One who doesn't leave you to try and just figure it out on your own, but rather comes alongside you gently, lovingly, wisely instructing you all along the way.

As a perfect teacher, the Spirit reminds us of God's goodness, power, and mercy. He reminds us of Christ's sacrifice for us. He reminds us that we are not alone. He teaches us from His Word. We can choose to be attentive students, or we can choose to ignore His instruction. What kind of student are you?

# Gardener

*I am the true vine, and my Father is the gardener.*
John 15:1

A good gardener doesn't just plant seeds and then leave them alone to make it on their own. No, a good gardener tends his garden—clipping, pruning, watering, and tenderly caring for his plants. I'm thankful that our Gardener, our heavenly Father, carefully and lovingly tends to our lives. We may not understand why we need something clipped or pruned, but we can trust our Gardener that He is doing it to strengthen us and help us grow to be even more fruitful and useful in His kingdom.

God wants us to bear fruit. He wants to bring a blessing to this world through our actions and words. He doesn't want us to live a meaningless life—rather, His desire is for us to bring good fruit to this world.

*Father, thank You for tending us as our Gardener. Thank You also for the pruning You do in our lives to help us bear more fruit. We want to be fruitful for You.*

# Vine

*I am the vine; you are the branches.*
JOHN 15:5

Jesus is the Vine; the one from whom we get nourishment and strength. We are nothing without Him. Yet if we remain in Him (abide in Him, dwell in Him) we will bear much fruit. God did not intend for us to try to live our lives independently of Him. Instead He wants us to be connected with Him, finding our life in Him. The Bible says the fruit of God's Spirit is love, joy, peace, patience, kindness, goodness, faithfulness, gentleness, and self-control. A woman with these qualities is a positive and beautiful woman, pointing people to the love of the Father.

The fruit of God's Spirit does not come naturally. These beautiful qualities are a result of abiding in Him and allowing His presence to fill your life. Our own efforts to be good and gentle and kind easily wither, but as we abide in Christ these qualities grow to produce abundant and delicious fruit, which brings nourishment to all around us. Look to Him, talk with Him, enjoy His presence throughout your day.

*He Is Our...*

# Friend

*I no longer call you servants ...*
*Instead, I have called you friends.*
JOHN 15:15

How can it be that our Lord and Master calls us His friends instead of His servants? Through faith in Christ we not only have a Savior, but a faithful Friend who will never leave us or forsake us. He loved us so much that He gave His life for us. Jesus said, "Greater love has no one than this: to lay down one's life for one's friends." Certainly we have the greatest Friend of all in Christ. What a privilege to know that we can fellowship with Him anytime and go to Him with our cares and concerns as well as our joy and thankfulness.

Jesus commanded us as His followers to love each other in the same way we have been loved by Him. Christ loves us with a sacrificial and forgiving love. Because we have been loved with such undeserved yet unending faithful love, we in turn can freely and sacrificially love others.

*He...*

# **Overcomes the World**

*In the world you will have tribulation; but be
of good cheer, I have overcome the world.*

JOHN 16:33 NKJV

Jesus didn't make any promises that our lives would be
smooth sailing. On the contrary, He said we would
have tribulation. Jesus spoke these words on the night
He was to be betrayed; the night of the Last Supper. He
knew He would be facing the cross, and He knew His
followers would be facing persecution. He gave them a
warning, but also a word of encouragement.

Be of good cheer? How could Jesus say that, with all
they were about to face? He could offer them encouragement because of one reason—He is the one who
overcomes the world. He wins! He knew He would
have victory over death and the grave, and He knew
He would have victory over the enemy. Through the
storms of life, we too can have peace and good cheer,
because we know He is able to overcome the world and
its encumbrances.

*He Is the...*

# Rabboni

*Mary turned toward him and cried out in*
*Aramaic, "Rabboni!" (which means "Teacher").*

JOHN 20:16

Mary used a Galilean term of respect toward Jesus that meant "Master." She humbly respected Jesus as her Master and Teacher. What a beautiful place to be, looking to Jesus as His student, recognizing that He had the words of life. Who is your master teacher? Often we get distracted and try to forge our way on our own, forgetting our Master and Teacher lovingly instructs those who have ears to hear.

As a follower of Christ, we learn from Him. We learn from His Word, and we learn from His example as we study both in Scripture. As His disciples or students we follow in His footsteps. My fellow student, are you hungry to learn from Him? Do you look to Him for instruction and guidance each day? He is not just a man we learn about in church; He is our Teacher, our Master, our Instructor for life.

*He Is the...*

# Holy One of God

*You will not abandon me to the realm of the dead,*
*you will not let your Holy One see decay.*

ACTS 2:26-27

Peter first recognized Jesus as the Holy One after Jesus performed a miracle of an overwhelming catch of fish. With the boat overflowing, Peter fell at Jesus' knees and said, "Oh, Lord, please leave me—I'm too much of a sinner to be around you." A humble recognition of Christ's holiness and his own sinfulness. In our passage today, we read Peter's speech as he taught the crowds at Pentecost. He quoted from one of David's psalms that prophetically portrayed Christ, the Holy One.

Recognizing Jesus as the Holy One changes who we are. Our reaction may be similar to Peter's, realizing our sinfulness and feeling unworthy to come near to a Holy God. But Jesus welcomes us into His arms. He is the Holy One, but He is also our Shepherd and our Friend. He responds to us as He did to Peter on the boat: "Don't be afraid; from now on you will fish for people."[84]

*He Is the...*

# Loving Father

*By him we cry, "Abba, Father."*
ROMANS 8:15

The Aramaic word for Father, *Abba*, does not imply a distant Father; rather, this word is a term of endearment. *Daddy* or *Papa* would be a more accurate translation. When we consider the holiness of God it is sometimes difficult to think of Him as our close and personal Father as well. Yet the Scripture is clear—we have been adopted into His family as sons and daughters.

In Psalms we are reminded that as a father has compassion on his children, so the Lord has compassion on those who fear Him. As Christians, when we pray to our Father, He lovingly welcomes us into His arms. He holds us in His safe arms through the storms of life and reassures us that He is in control. Do not be afraid to bring your requests to your Daddy who loves you.

# Patient

*May the God of patience and comfort grant you
to be like-minded toward one another.*

ROMANS 15:5 NKJV

Aren't you thankful for God's patience with us? He is patient and slow to anger when it comes to our sins and mistakes. He is a God of endurance. He does not speed up our learning process, but allows us to learn and grow slowly and surely. He is not quick to be frustrated with us, but rather offers both His patience and comfort to us.

As recipients of His kind comfort and patient endurance with us, ought we not also to have this same kind of endurance and kindness toward others? It may seem hard, if not impossible, to be patient with some people in our lives, whether co-workers, family members, or neighbors. It is wonderful to know that we can go to the God of patience and comfort and seek His help. Thank Him daily for His patience and comfort toward you. It will serve as a reminder that as we have received, let us freely give!

# Fills Us with Joy and Peace

*May the God of hope fill you with all joy
and peace as you trust in him.*

ROMANS 15:13

Joy and peace—what tremendous qualities for any person to possess. We all want to be around joyful and peaceful people, but doesn't it seem as though few people actually experience it? Yet, there is hope from the God of hope. He is the one who fills us with joy and peace when we trust Him. When our eyes are focused on our circumstances or our hurts or worries, then our joy and peace diminish greatly, but when our eyes are on the God of hope we experience a divine sense of joy and peace.

As we trust Him, we remember that He loves us and that with Him all things are possible. Instead of worrying, we find a peace that passes all understanding when we turn our eyes toward Him. What may seem sorrowful in our lives can grow into a deeper sense of eternal joy as we trust that He can use our trials for a greater purpose.

# Last Adam

*The first man Adam became a living being;*
*the last Adam, a life-giving spirit.*

1 CORINTHIANS 15:45

In his letter to the Corinthians, Paul contrasts the first Adam (the first man in the Garden of Eden), with the Last Adam (Christ Jesus). Sin and death entered the world through the first Adam, yet life and forgiveness entered the world through the Last Adam—Jesus. The first Adam took away life; the Last Adam gave life. It was because of the first Adam that the Last Adam had to come.

We can relate to the first Adam, as we are human and sinful. We face decay and death in our human bodies, but the Last Adam came to bring us hope and life. One day we will have a new and glorified body in eternity. Although the first Adam introduced death to the world, the Last Adam introduced the promise of victory over death. Christ, the Last Adam, overcame death through His resurrection.

*He Is a...*

# Comforter

*... Father of compassion and the God of all comfort.*
2 Corinthians 1:3

When life's difficulties come our way, we need comfort. How wonderful to know that the God of all creation is also a God of comfort. He desires to bring comfort to His people. He does not want to bring harm, but rather consolation. He sent Christ as the consolation of Israel to save us from the wages of our sin. He sent His Spirit as our Helper, our Counselor, our Advocate. He is able to console us in our pain, our sorrows, and our weaknesses.

The God of all comfort never leaves His people. You are not alone in your sorrows, for the Bible reminds us He is close to the brokenhearted. The work of His Spirit is to strengthen and encourage our hearts and minds. He helps us in so many ways. He brings comfort through other people, through His Word, through circumstances, and sometimes through His gentle voice comforting our spirit. Allow Him to comfort you as you face the frustrations of each day or as you walk through the darkest valley. He is close beside you.

*He...*

# Shines His Light

*God, who said, "Let there be light in the darkness,"
has made this light shine in our hearts.*

2 Corinthians 4:6

God spoke light into darkness when He created the universe, and He is the same God who shines His light into our darkened hearts. Paul wrote that God shined His light "so we could know the glory of God that is seen in the face of Jesus Christ." Without His illuminating our eyes we would not have recognized Jesus. God in His kindness allowed His light to shine in our hearts so we could see His Son.

His light opens our spiritual eyes so we can see His truth. As we read His Word, let us ask Him to shine His light so we can understand His truth. As we walk through our day, let us ask Him to shine His light on our path so we may walk in wisdom and discernment. As we share the gospel with others, let us be diligent to ask the Lord to shine His light on the heart of the unbeliever.

*Father, thank You for Your light, which shines brightly in our hearts.*

*He...*

# Never Abandons Us

*We are hunted down, but never abandoned by God.*
2 CORINTHIANS 4:9 NLT

Paul and his team lived under the constant threat of persecution for preaching Christ. In addition to being hunted down, Paul wrote that they were "pressed on every side by troubles, but we are not crushed. We are perplexed, but not driven to despair...knocked down, but we are not destroyed." Paul knew that he would never be abandoned by the Lord, who was his strength in troubled times.

How was Paul able to stick with it and not lose heart? Later in this very same passage we find his answer: "We don't look at the troubles we can see now; rather, we fix our gaze on things that cannot be seen. For the things we see now will soon be gone, but the things we cannot see will last forever." My friend, fix your focus on the God who is eternal and will never abandon you. He will give you the endurance and strength to carry on.

*He...*

# Makes Us New

*If anyone is in Christ, the new creation has come:*
*The old has gone, the new is here!*

2 CORINTHIANS 5:17

God changes us. He transforms us from our old, self-centered, sinful, guilty creatures to beautiful new creations. He cleans out our self-centered sinfulness and gives us the power to turn from sin and live a God-centered life. He gives us His divine nature because His Spirit dwells within us. We are no longer slaves to sin, but rather we are a part of His royal family.

God is not finished working on us. I find it comforting to know we are works in progress. Paul wrote to the Philippians, "I am certain that God, who began the good work within you, will continue his work until it is finally finished on the day when Christ Jesus returns."[85] Aren't you thankful that God has not only made us new, but will continue His work until the day we see Him face-to-face? He is always at work in our lives, transforming us and conforming us to His Son's image.

*He Gives...*
# Grace

*You know the grace of our Lord Jesus Christ, that*
*though he was rich, yet for your sake he became poor,*
*so that you through his poverty might become rich.*

2 CORINTHIANS 8:9

Grace. What a beautiful word—divine favor, unde-served gift. Those who believe in Christ are the recipients of God's redemptive mercy and grace. What greater joy can there be than to know we have received such a gift? We could not pay our own debt, but Christ became poor, leaving His heavenly place so that we might be made rich in grace.

We could not save ourselves, yet God in His loving-kindness made a way for us to be forgiven. It is not what we have done, but what Christ did for us on the cross. Spurgeon said, "Thou hast need of nothing beyond what there is in Him. In Him thou art at this moment just, in Him entirely clean, in Him an object of divine approval and eternal love."[86] Rejoice in His grace.

*He Shows His...*

# Power in Our Weakness

*My grace is sufficient for you,*
*for my power is made perfect in weakness.*
2 Corinthians 12:9

When you think of power, what comes to mind? Maybe you think about the power of a storm or the power of electricity. Perhaps power tools or power equipment or even the power of muscles. But the power referred to in this verse is not like any power we know here on earth. The Greek word for power in this verse, *dunamis,* indicates a supernatural power. *Dunamis* typically refers to forces from a higher realm that have entered and are working in this lower world of ours.

The power God gives us in our weakness is not like the power we see displayed by nature or other familiar things. It is beyond us. Like Paul, we can glory in our weaknesses knowing that they offer the perfect opportunity for God's supernatural power to do a mighty work through us.

*He Acts According to His...*

# Good Pleasure

*He made known to us the mystery*
*of his will according to his good pleasure.*
EPHESIANS 1:9

Good pleasure? What is God's good pleasure? It means that He has a good plan that He has always purposed to carry out. He is good, and His plans are good. At first glance some things that happen to us may not seem so good, or even good at all, yet He can bring good from even difficult situations. In Romans we are reminded that He works all things together for the good for those who love Him and are called according to His purpose.

Our scripture today says that it was God's good pleasure to make known the mystery of His will. He has graciously allowed us to know the mystery of Christ. His plan throughout the ages was to send Christ. And what a good plan it was! Jesus' cruel death on the cross didn't seem good at the time, but it was God's good pleasure to offer salvation to this world. Let us trust in His good pleasure, for His plans are perfect.

# **Rich in Mercy**

*Because of his great love for us, God,
who is rich in mercy, made us alive with Christ.*

EPHESIANS 2:4-5

Aren't you glad that our God is overflowing and wealthy when it comes to mercy? He is not stingy in His great love and compassion toward us. We were destitute in our own sinfulness, but the One who is rich in mercy made us alive in Christ. We are spiritually rich indeed.

Since we have been shown such mercy, we also ought to be rich in mercy toward others. We may not have wealth in other areas, but this is one area in which we can choose to be rich as we show compassion toward the people around us. We can overflow with mercy by looking for ways we can bless and help others who cannot help themselves. It may mean giving our time to help a neighbor, it could mean forgiving someone who made a mistake, or it may mean bringing a meal to someone who is in need. Ask the Lord, who is rich in mercy, to open your eyes and help you to express His mercy to others.

# Chief Cornerstone

*... Christ Jesus himself as the chief cornerstone.*
EPHESIANS 2:20

A cornerstone (also known as a "foundation stone") in Jesus' day was the first stone set in the construction of a building's foundation. It was of vital importance because all other stones were set in reference to it. The cornerstone essentially determined the position, squareness, and levelness of the entire structure. In the same way, the foundation of our lives should be built on Christ. He sets the direction and the position of our lives. Our lives can be built with purpose and meaning with Him as the foundation stone.

As followers of Christ we not only have Him as our cornerstone, but we choose to actively build our lives on Him. We must ask ourselves, What kind of structure am I building? Am I looking to Him as my principal stone, the one who sets the tone and direction for my life as my reference point? With our hearts and minds anchored in Him, our lives can withstand the storms of life, for He is a sure foundation.

# Over All, Through All, in All

*One God and Father of all, who is over
all and through all and in all.*

Ephesians 4:6

As Paul described the body of believers in Christ he said, "There is one body and one Spirit...one Lord, one faith, one baptism." God is the One who is over all, through all, and in all believers. What a marvelous blessing! The same Spirit that is in you as a follower of Christ is also in me and in our brothers and sisters in the faith. We are connected on a spiritual level. We should all function as one body in Christ.

There is great power indicated by this statement, for if God is over all, through all, and in all, His divine power dwells mightily in us. It is amazing to think of us as not only partakers of His grace but recipients of His divine nature. Let us live as one body, connected by our common bond of His Spirit alive within us. He is the authority over us, the love through us, and the power within us.

*Praise You, Father, for being our all in all.*

# Name Above Every Name

*God exalted him to the highest place
and gave him the name that is above every name.*

PHILIPPIANS 2:9

What is in a name? Our names identify us and distinguish us from one another. Jesus' name holds power and life. Jesus humbled Himself by giving His life for us on the cross. Philippians tells us that He did not grasp or cling to His heavenly rights, but willingly came to offer His life for us. Therefore, God exalted Him to the highest place. He also gave Him the name that is above every name.

Jesus' name is above all others. No person has a greater name. There is no angel that has a greater name. In heaven and on earth, we can find no name greater than His. Other religions may claim that there are other deities equal or greater. We know that Jesus' name is over every other name. His followers represent His name. May we never dishonor His name—rather, let us be diligent to bring honor and glory to Him in our words and actions.

*He...*

# Works in Us

*It is God who works in you to will
and to act in order to fulfill his good purpose.*

PHILIPPIANS 2:13

God is always at work. He is not lazy, nor does He fall asleep on the job. In fact the psalmist reminds us that "the one who watches over you will not slumber."[87] Our passage today reminds us that He is at work in us. In his letter to the Philippians Paul also wrote that, "He who began a good work in you will carry it on to completion until the day of Christ Jesus." God is at work in our lives, and His work is not finished yet.

Isn't it amazing to think that the God of all creation is continually working in us? He loves us and has given us His Spirit. He is working in us both to will and to act in order to fulfill His good purpose. And He is constantly at work in us giving us not only the ability but the desire to fulfill that purpose. I'm glad God doesn't give up on us. He is always at work.

# All-Sufficient One

*My God will meet all your needs according
to the riches of his glory in Christ Jesus.*

PHILIPPIANS 4:19

God is sufficient unto Himself. His glorious riches never run dry. He does not have needs, nor does He depend on anyone. He is not needy, but He invites those in need to find their strength in Him. He is able to supply all our needs according to His glorious riches in Christ Jesus. As believers, we have the Lord as our Shepherd and we have all that we need.

He is our sufficient one. Unlike Him, we have needs and we cannot meet all of them. Our greatest need is a spiritual hunger that no one can satisfy except God alone. He fulfills our need. We have been given fullness in Christ and are satisfied in Him. Where do you look for fulfillment? My dear sister, go to the All-Sufficient One. He is able to satisfy your every longing according to His glorious and eternal riches.

# Firstborn over All Creation

*The Son is the image of the invisible God,
the firstborn over all creation.*

COLOSSIANS 1:15

In the first century, the term *firstborn* referred to the one who is the highest ranking in authority, the chief, the heir with the greatest privilege and responsibility. In the context of their own families, the Jewish people of Jesus' day honored the firstborn with the greatest rights, a double inheritance, and a privileged position. Certainly they had a deep sense of respect for the firstborn.

What are the implications of Jesus being the firstborn over all creation? It means that He is the supreme one and highest authority over all that is created. He is the exact image of the invisible God, above all creation. The term *firstborn* does not imply that He was born, but rather that He is above all creation. He Himself was not created for He has always existed. Paul also proclaimed that Jesus was the "firstborn from among the dead."[88] Again as we look at the meaning of the term we see that Jesus Himself was the one who triumphed over death, gaining the promise of eternal life for us all. Let us worship Him as the triumphant one, the supreme authority over the living and the dead. To Him be glory and honor and power.

*He Is Our...*

# Sustainer

*He is before all things, and in him all things hold together.*
COLOSSIANS 1:17

When life seems to be falling apart, we know the One who can hold us together. He is not only our Creator, but He is also our Sustainer. He holds the universe together, He holds this world together, and He holds our lives together. Things may seem chaotic at times, but the God who sees all has us in His hands. Nothing is out of control as far as He is concerned, because through Him all things exist and consist.

When we face tragedies or difficulties it is easy to think that God has let everything fall apart, but it is in the dark moments that our faith grows stronger as we trust the Sustainer of life. He is not surprised by our situation, nor has He allowed something to fall out of His hands. Trust His plan even when you don't understand it, and rest in His loving and tender hands as He holds you together.

*He Is the…*

# Head of the Body

*He is the head of the body, the church.*
Colossians 1:18

C hrist is the head, the authoritative leader, of the church. He is central to its existence and direction, just as a head is essential for a human body to function and exist. Those who have placed their faith in Him and follow Him are the church or the body of Christ. As His body, we depend on Him, but we also have a variety of responsibilities and functions in order to work together properly and effectively. Paul encouraged the members of the body of Christ to grow in Him and not remain in a state of infancy.

He wrote to the Ephesians,

> We will grow to become in every respect the mature body of him who is the head, that is, Christ. From him the whole body, joined and held together by every supporting ligament, grows and builds itself up in love, as each part does its work. [89]

Let us consider the work (gifts and talents) God has given us and work together to strengthen the body of Christ.

# **Mystery of God**

*That they may know the mystery of God, namely, Christ.*
COLOSSIANS 2:2

The word *mystery* comes from the Greek word *musterion*, meaning "secret." Among the ancient Greeks, mysteries were religious rites and ceremonies practiced by secret societies. Those who were initiated into these mysteries became possessors of secret knowledge and were called "The Perfected." Paul wanted believers in Christ to understand that the full riches of complete understanding were found in Jesus alone. The mystery of God *is* Christ, not some obscure knowledge from a secret society.

Christ is the secret that unlocks the door to salvation. He is the one who gives us spiritual wisdom and understanding. We need not look beyond Him for the way to God. He revealed the Father to us; He made a way for us to eternal life through the cross. Some may be enticed to chase after secret knowledge, but we know that the mystery of God is found in Christ.

# **Treasures of Wisdom and Knowledge**

*... Christ, in whom are hidden all the
treasures of wisdom and knowledge.*

COLOSSIANS 2:3

The world is full of treasure-seekers. Some try to find their treasures in the pursuit of money and a large bank account. Others seek treasures through having a beautiful house or expensive cars. There are those who seek treasures in having the perfect body or perfect kids or perfect life. Yet these treasures never seem to satisfy. There is always a desire for more because they are hollow and temporary, not lasting.

Where do you look for treasure? In Christ we discover all the treasures of wisdom and knowledge, and those who find Him are spiritually wealthy indeed! Jesus said, "Where your heart is there is your treasure also." Christ is our true and lasting treasure. Let us find our heart's satisfaction in Him.

*Father, thank You for Christ, our true treasure. May we continually find our strength and joy in Him.*

*In Him Lives...*

# All the Fullness of the Deity

*In Christ all the fullness of the Deity lives in bodily form.*
COLOSSIANS 2:9

All God; all man. Jesus was both fully God and fully human. In Paul's day, the early Gnostic influence caused some to be confused about Christ. Basically the Gnostics believed that anything of the spirit was pure and good, while anything material—of the flesh—was innately evil. They couldn't fathom how a good God could possibly come in the flesh. Paul proclaimed clearly here that, yes, Jesus was God and He was also human.

Why is this important? Because Jesus is the mediator between God and man. He was the perfect sacrifice because He was both man and God. In today's world, people still speculate as to who Christ is. As believers in Him, we must stand confidently on the foundation that Jesus was all God and all human. There is no one else who can make that claim.

*He Is the...*

# Head over Every
# Power and Authority

*You have been given fullness in Christ,*
*who is the head over every power and authority.*

COLOSSIANS 2:10

Not only is Christ the Head of the body, which is the church, He is Ruler over every power and authority. Ultimately everyone answers to Him, whether on this earth or beyond this world. He is Head over kings and over angels. He is Ruler over all, yet He came to serve. He can command angels to come to His rescue, yet He willingly gave His life for us.

We have been given fullness in Him. We are fulfilled, satisfied, complete in the One who is above all others. Isn't that magnificent? The One who is Head over every power and authority also completes our life. We have no need for more than what we have received from Christ. As Head over all, He has defeated sin and death.

*All praise to God our Father, and to the Lord Jesus, who is Head over every power and authority. We worship You, our King.*

# Seated at the Right Hand of the Father

*Set your hearts on things above,*
*where Christ is, seated at the right hand of God.*

COLOSSIANS 3:1

hrist is seated at the right hand of God in a place of honor, power, and authority. This is the place reserved for the most honored One. As those who have been redeemed by Him, we are to set our hearts on things above, the place where Christ is. All too often our hearts are drawn and enticed by the pleasures and interests of this world. We often seek what we can have now, not what we have to look forward to in heaven.

How can we be deliberate about turning our hearts and affections toward things above? It begins by setting our minds on things above—getting to know who Christ is through knowing what the Bible says about Him. Most important, as we simply enjoy His presence, reflecting on Him and what He has done, our hearts grow affectionate toward Him. Let us set our hearts toward our wonderful Lord moment by moment each day.

# Your Life

*When Christ, who is your life, appears,
then you also will appear with him in glory.*

COLOSSIANS 3:4

Christ is not just a part of our life as His followers or a nice guy that we compartmentalize to Sunday mornings. He *is* our life. He is in us, He lives through us. He gives us strength and wisdom for our journey. Most important, He gives us the promise of eternal life. He is the one who makes us who we are. He is our life, and without Him our lives would be incomplete and without purpose.

Our verse today is filled with great promise. It not only reminds us that our life is abundantly fulfilled and enriched here on this earth through Christ, but we also have the beautiful promise that He will appear again. When He appears, we will also appear with Him in glory. We are reassured in Scripture that He will return one day, and when He does we will be with Him in glory.

# All and in All

*Christic is all, and is in all.*
COLOSSIANS 3:11

As we unpack this wonderful treasure of a verse, we must first recognize that Paul was addressing believers. His purpose was to help them see that there were no distinctions in God's eyes between Jews or Greeks, slave or free, circumcised or uncircumcised. It's not what is on the outside as far as status or heritage; it's what is on the inside. If you are a follower of Christ, His Spirit dwells within you. It is an amazing truth to grasp—that the Spirit of the living God lives inside us. He is in all believers. What a uniting factor for the body of Christ!

He is our all. Christ is our all because He paid it all on the cross. He is all we need. He is the one who has allowed us to stand forgiven before a Holy God. He is our all. Without Him we would be dead in our sins. My fellow follower of Christ, let us rejoice that Christ is all that we need for salvation, and that He is in all who believe.

# Came to Save Sinners

*Christ Jesus came into the world to save sinners.*
1 Timothy 1:15

Jesus left His throne in heaven to come to this earth to save sinners. Paul humbly adds, "Of whom I am the worst." The great and powerful apostle Paul recognized his own sin and his own desperate need for a savior. This is the beginning step for each of us in coming to Christ. If we do not recognize our sin, we do not recognize our need to be saved. He came to save sinners, not perfect people (or people who think they are without sin).

The Bible reminds us that all have sinned and fallen short of God's glory. We cannot enter heaven and live with a holy God unless our sin problem is resolved. God sent a way for sinners to be saved from eternal punishment through His beloved Son, Jesus. The very name of Jesus—*Yeshua* in Hebrew—means "Jehovah is salvation."

*Father, we praise You for sending Jesus to save us. We confess our sin and recognize our need for Him.*

*He Is the...*

# Invisible God

*To the King eternal, immortal, invisible,
the only God, be honor and glory.*

1 Timothy 1:17

God the Father is immortal and invisible. Although no one has seen the Father, Jesus has made Him known to us. He is God incarnate—God in the flesh, or in human form. Jesus Himself declared, "No one has ever seen God, but the one and only Son, who is himself God and is in closest relationship with the Father, has made him known."[90] Jesus made the invisible God visible to mankind. In Him we see the very nature of God. We see His grace, mercy, love, and patience. We see His holiness.

Although we cannot see God, we can see evidence of His handiwork and power all around us. Just as we cannot actually see the wind, but we can see evidence that it is there through the ripples on the water or the rustling of the leaves in the trees, so we see God's fingerprints in the world He created.

# **Mediator**

*There is one God and one mediator between
God and mankind, the man Christ Jesus.*

1 TIMOTHY 2:5

When two parties are at odds they need a mediator, a reconciler, one who will go between them and bring peace. Christ Jesus is the mediator between a holy God and sinful men. He is the only One who could act as the mediator, because He alone was sinless. The salvation of man required a perfect sacrifice. Our verse today reminds us that there are not many possible mediators between God and man—there is just one, Christ Jesus.

On our own, we cannot appease a perfect God. The chasm is too wide. There are irreconcilable differences between a holy God and sinful man, and the only way they can be brought together is through one who is both God and man.

*Lord, we praise You for making it possible for us to experience peace with You. Thank You for sending Your mediator so that we may no longer be enemies, but rather be a part of Your family.*

*He...*

# Does Not Lie

*... a faith and knowledge resting on the hope
of eternal life, which God, who does not
lie, promised before the beginning of time.*

Titus 1:2

We can trust God's Word, for He does not lie. His promises are sure and can be depended upon. His word is true and is our sure foundation. In a world permeated with deceit and dishonesty, it is wonderful to know we can trust His word. He is sure and true. If you are searching for truth, you will find it in God, for He does not lie. Indeed, God's Son, Jesus, is the Truth, and we know that we find our true way to God as we trust in Him.

Satan is the father of lies and deceit. He often deceives using half-truths. He cannot be trusted, and his lies distract us from the truth. God, on the other hand, does not tell partial truths. We can completely trust His Word and His ways. God's Spirit guides us toward the truth, so continue to walk with Him. Search the Bible for God's promises and hold on to them. Depend on them, for He does not lie.

# Exact Representation
# of the Father

*The Son is the radiance of God's glory
and the exact representation of his being.*

HEBREWS 1:3

The Bible leaves no question about who Jesus is. He was not just a good man or a prophet, or a good example for us to follow. He is the radiance of God's glory, the sole expression of a mighty and holy God. The word "radiance" actually means a brightness or a shining forth of light coming from a luminous body. It is not a reflected brightness, but rather a brightness shining forth from Him. The Light of the world.

He is the exact representation, not merely a partial replica or something "sort of like" the original. This unique description of Jesus indicates that the person of Jesus is distinct from the Father and yet literally equal to God. He is the imprint, the image or "impress" of God's essence. The fact that He sustains all things by His powerful Word shows that He has the authority to do all things. The writer of Hebrews leaves no room for doubt—Jesus is God.

*He Is Our...*

# High Priest

*Fix your thoughts on Jesus, whom we acknowledge
as our apostle and high priest.*

HEBREWS 3:1

In the Old Testament, the high priest was God's appointed person to represent the people to Himself. Every high priest had the job of offering gifts and sacrifices to God in order to intercede for the sins of the people. He was a mediator between the Israelites and God.

We now have a permanent High Priest. Jesus is the one whom God appointed to mediate between Himself, holy God, and sinful man, offering the sacrifice of His own life. Hebrews reminds us,

> We do not have a high priest who is unable to empathize with our weaknesses, but we have one who has been tempted in every way, just as we are—yet he did not sin. Let us then approach God's throne of grace with confidence, so that we may receive mercy and find grace to help us in our time of need.[91]

We can come boldly before the Lord because we have a merciful High Priest. He understands us and knows ours needs. Oh, what joy to know that our High Priest loves us and welcomes us to His throne of grace!

# Word Is Alive and Powerful

*The word of God is alive and active.*

HEBREWS 4:12

God's Word, the Bible, is not like any other book. It is a treasure filled with wisdom and knowledge. You may read a book now and then that moves you or motivates you, but God's Word will literally transform your life. It is not dead—rather, it is alive and active. Hebrews goes on to describe it as, "Sharper than any double-edged sword, it penetrates even to dividing soul and spirit, joints and marrow; it judges the thoughts and attitudes of the heart." Now that's a powerful book!

Let us read it, study it, and meditate upon it with reverence and care. Prayerfully ask the Lord to teach you as you read its pages. There is great joy, powerful wisdom, and loving conviction to be found in the Bible. Let us feed on its living truth every day to nourish and strengthen our soul. His Word is not dead, but very much alive!

*He Was Our...*

# Ransom

*He has died as a ransom to set them free from
the sins committed under the first covenant.*

HEBREWS 9:15

Whenever there is a kidnapping, the captor demands a ransom. Sin is a cruel captor. Not only does it ruin our lives, trapping us in negative behaviors, but it demands a high price for a ransom. We could not pay it ourselves. Only one person could—God's only Son. We have been bought with a price. Completely paid for. Christ is our ransom, who offered His life on the cross on our behalf.

He paid the price that we would no longer be slaves to our sins. His death on the cross paid the price in full. Our scripture today reminds us that those whom He called to Himself, those of us who have received His invitation, receive the promise of eternal life. What a glorious inheritance we have—set free from sin, ransomed by God's own Son—so that one day we will live with Him in glory.

*He Is the...*

# **Author and Finisher of Our Faith**

*Looking unto Jesus, the author and finisher of our faith.*
HEBREWS 12:1-2 NKJV

Jesus is the originator of our faith. He wrote our faith into our hearts and into His book. He is the divine Author of our lives, and without His authorship we would not have faith in Him. We would be a blank slate, not believing or understanding all that God has done and can do. The Bible says that we were dead in our sins, but God has made us alive with Christ.[92] Isn't it a wonderful thought that our Creator penned our faith with His own hand? He wrote our story and our faith journey.

He is also the completer of our faith; the one who finishes the story. He sees us through this life here on earth and on into eternity. In Him we are made perfect and complete, not lacking anything. Knowing He is the creator and completer of our faith makes us want to set aside the sin that entangles us. With our eyes on Him we have the endurance to run our race of faith, knowing He is running with us from start to finish.

# Disciplines

*The Lord disciplines the one he loves,*
*and he chastens everyone he accepts as his son.*
HEBREWS 12:6

If a parent loves his children, he will discipline them to help them learn to turn from what is wrong and walk the joyful path of righteousness. The word for "discipline" (Greek *paideia*) actually means the training or instruction of a child. Discipline is healthy and is vital to our well-being and growth as a person. Without it we would wander down dangerous paths. Our Father loves us and cares for us, and therefore He corrects and trains us for our own protection.

We must never conclude that every bad thing in our lives is the Lord's discipline. The Lord allows difficulties in our lives for a number of reasons, but there are times when He is specifically correcting us. Let us be good students and learn from His careful and loving instruction. Do not despise or make light of His discipline—rather, live with an attitude of "What can I learn from this?"

# Cannot Be Tempted

*God cannot be tempted by evil, nor does he tempt anyone.*
JAMES 1:13

God is above temptation. He is holy and has no capacity for evil. Nothing pulls or leads Him astray. He doesn't get distracted by evil like we do. He also doesn't tempt anyone. That's Satan's work, not God's. No one can claim that God tempted them. In the case of Job, we saw that He allowed Satan to bring trials into Job's life. God allows trials in our lives, and He uses them for certain purposes, often to strengthen us and cause us to mature. On the other hand, He does not tempt us or deliberately entice us toward evil.

James goes on to write that "each person is tempted when they are dragged away by their own evil desire and enticed." We cannot blame our temptations on God, but we can go to Him, the One who is not tempted by evil, and ask for His help. Let us ask Him to help us to have good desires and a clean heart so we may honor Him and not fall into temptation.

*He Is...*

# Unchanging

*Every good and perfect gift is from above,
coming down from the Father of the heavenly
lights, who does not change like shifting shadows.*
JAMES 1:17

Circumstances and people may change, but God does not change. We can find strength in the fact that our God is unchanging and immutable. He can be depended upon as our rock, and He can be trusted as our refuge. We who are ever-changing need a God who does not change like shifting shadows. He does not need to change, for He is already complete—perfect—with no room for improvement.

Just as much as God's unchangeableness is a wonderful and endearing quality, it is also wonderful to know that *we* can change. We do not need to stay the same; we can always improve, learn, grow, and get better. The unchangeable God is able to change us for the better. He gives us the choice to make positive changes or negative ones in our lives. Let us look to Him to help us make wise decisions toward positive changes in our lives.

# Perfect Judge

*God alone, who gave the law, is the Judge.*
*He alone has the power to save or to destroy.*
*So what right do you have to judge your neighbor?*
JAMES 4:12 NLT

James admonished the early church, "Don't speak evil against each other, dear brothers and sisters. If you criticize and judge each other, then you are criticizing and judging God's law." Gossip, slander, and criticism destroy the unity we have in the body of Christ. We must guard against using our mouths to tear people down. We need to build others up with our words and leave the judging to God.

It's easy to become critical of others, and sometime we even think it is our job to point out the faults and shortcomings of our brothers and sisters. Remember that God alone is the Judge. Jesus said, "Do not judge others, and you will not be judged."[93] Certainly we must be discerning, but we must also recognize we are not the ultimate judge. Get rid of the critical spirit, replace it with love, and leave the judging up to God.

# **Triune God**

*... according to the foreknowledge of God the Father,*
*through the sanctifying work of the Spirit,*
*to be obedient to Jesus Christ and sprinkled with his blood.*
1 PETER 1:1-2

The concept of the Trinity is impossible for our finite minds to grasp. Three distinct Persons yet one God—the Holy Trinity is mysterious and beyond our comprehension. We see various pictures in nature that help us get our minds around the concept of the Trinity. Take water, for instance. We find water in the form of a solid (ice), a liquid, and a vapor (steam). All of these are $H_2O$, yet in three different forms. Certainly the "living water" that Jesus offers is far more wonderful than this simple analogy, but this picture helps us in a small way to understand three-in-one.

From our passage today we see the work of the triune God in the believer's life. God the Father knew us and called us to Himself, Christ died for us, and the Holy Spirit continues to do a sanctifying and cleansing work in us. Although we do not fully understand the concept of the Trinity, we can fully accept and rejoice in the work He does in our lives.

*He Is the...*

# **Overseer of Your Soul**

*Now you have returned to the Shepherd
and Overseer of your souls.*

1 PETER 2:25

Jesus is the Guardian of our souls. He oversees and cares for our eternal well-being. Before we came to know Christ we were like sheep going astray. We followed our own path without looking to God for help, guidance, or salvation. But now that we know Christ, things are different. We have One who watches over us and who cares about what happens to us. Jesus is not indifferent to us, nor does He ignore us like a lazy shepherd. On the contrary, we have His constant attention, and He cares about the very essence of who we are; He cares for our souls.

As His followers we can be confident that He will guard us and keep us safe from the enemy's grasp. We are in safe care, as our souls are watched over by Christ.

*Father, thank You for allowing us to know Jesus, the Overseer of our souls. We rejoice in the safety of Your care.*

*He...*
# Calls Us to Himself

*His divine power has given us everything we need*
*for a godly life through our knowledge of him*
*who called us by his own glory and goodness.*

2 PETER 1:3

God calls us to Himself. His divine invitation is for us to partake in the blessings of redemption. We do not want to ignore His invitation. It is because of His glory and goodness (not ours) that He has called us to Himself. When we accept His invitation to follow Him, He gives us everything we need to live a godly life. We receive all this by coming to know Him. That word *know* is not just a distant knowing, as if to just know about someone. It means to seek after Him, to investigate Him, to be connected.

It is not in a distant way that God calls us, but a close and intimate way. He is not simply an acquaintance sending us a random invitation. He is an intimate friend who lovingly calls us into a deep and abiding fellowship with Him. Accept His invitation to come and abide with Him. He loves you and will welcome you with outstretched arms.

# Not Slow in Keeping His Promise

*The Lord is not slow in keeping his promise,*
*as some understand slowness.*

2 PETER 3:9

God is slow to anger, but He is not slow when it comes to keeping His promise to return. He is waiting patiently for as many to come to redemption as will come. Peter reminds his readers that with the Lord, a thousand years is like a day and a day like a thousand years. Peter wrote this to reassure believers that Christ would come again as He promised. He warned that some would scoff, "Where is this coming he (Jesus) promised?"

Patiently, lovingly, God is waiting. Aren't you glad He isn't like us? We want everything now, now, now, but He is patient. Fools rush in; God waits. What may seem like "forever" to us is only an opportunity for more to come to repentance. He is not limited by our time frames. If you have been waiting for answers from Him, trust His wisdom in all things. He is timeless and knows exactly what He is doing.

*Father, we trust Your timing in every aspect of our lives.*

# Does Not Want Anyone to Perish

*He is patient with you, not wanting anyone to perish, but everyone to come to repentance.*

2 PETER 3:9

There are those who question, "How could a loving God allow people to perish in hell?" The question we should be asking is, "How can a holy God allow sinful people to approach Him and dwell with Him in eternity?" The beautiful answer is that God doesn't want anyone to perish, so He provided a way through His Son Jesus. God wants everyone to come to repentance, turn from their sins, and follow Jesus. The Bible tells us that he who has the Son has life, but he who does not have the Son does not have eternal life.

Lovingly and kindly God waits for all who will repent. He wants everyone who will believe to come to that point of belief. Perishing is not His desire for anyone. Life is His desire, and He offers it willingly and freely for all who will receive.

*Glorious Father, thank You that You don't want anyone to perish. Thank You for providing a way through Jesus.*

# **Lavishes His Love on Us**

*See what great love the Father has lavished
on us, that we should be called children
of God! And that is what we are!*

1 JOHN 3:1

Lavishly loved! That is what you are. Just as an adoring father lavishes his love on his children, so the Lord lavishes His great love, His perfect love, on us. Isn't it wonderful to be called His children? Children of the Most High God. That is what we are! How does a beloved daughter respond to an adoring daddy? She wants to please Him. She wants to spend time with Him. She wants to adore Him in response.

My dear sister, I long for you to see that your heavenly Father lavishes His great love on you. We so easily fall into the trap of guilt, or somehow thinking that God hates us. Through faith in Christ we are His children, and He adores us. Take time today to picture yourself wrapped in His loving arms, enjoying His warm embrace, and adoring Him as your loving Father.

# Showed Us What Love Is

*This is how we know what love is:*
*Jesus Christ laid down his life for us.*

1 JOHN 3:16

One song says, "I want to know what love is," while another song proclaims that "all we need is love." We know that our world needs love, but what does true love look like? Who really demonstrates true love? Our passage today reminds us that Jesus shows us exactly what love looks like. If you want to know what love is, here it is in a nutshell: Jesus laid down His life for us. He left all His heavenly rights and comforts and came to this earth in the form of a servant. He didn't demand His rights, but willingly subjected Himself to unrighteous men.

If we are to love others with a Jesus-type love, then we ought to willingly lay down our rights and serve each other. True love doesn't cling to its own rights nor does it demand its own way. God demonstrated His love for us in that while we were sinners, Christ died for us.

*He Is...*

# Love

*Everyone who loves has been born
of God and knows God.
Whoever does not love does not know
God, because God is love.*

1 John 4:7-8

God's very nature is love. When we look at the description of love in 1 Corinthians 13 we see a description of His very essence. He is patient, He is kind, He does not envy, He does not boast, He is not rude, He is not selfish, He is not easily angered, He keeps no record of wrongs for those who follow Him. He does not delight in evil but rejoices in the truth. He demonstrated His love through sending His Son Jesus to die on the cross on our behalf. Greater love has no man than this, that a man lay down his life for his friends.

Love is more than merely a feeling. It is a choice, an action, and a demonstration of self-sacrificing care for another. How well do you love others? Remember that love comes from God. Ask Him to pour His divine love through you as you reach out and patiently and self-lessly love those around you.

# Able to Keep You from Falling

*To him who is able to keep you from falling
and to present you before his glorious presence
without fault and with great joy.*

JUDE 24

What a glorious truth—He is able to keep us from falling. He is able to keep us from falling into a pit of self-destruction. He is able to keep us from falling into sin. In Psalms we are reminded that the Lord directs the steps of the righteous and delights in every detail of their lives. Though they stumble, they will not fall, for He holds them by the hand. Will you allow God to take your hand and hold you up when you are stumbling?

If we stumble, we know we will not fall into eternal punishment because of the cross of Christ. Because of His sacrifice for us, He is able to present us before God's glorious presence without fault. Don't you love how Jude adds "with great joy"? Jesus takes great joy in presenting us to the Father. Can't you just picture the joyful smile on His face as He introduces us to the Father as His beloved ones?

*He Is the...*

# Amen

*To the angel of the church in Laodicea write:*
*"These are the words of the Amen, the faithful*
*and true witness, the ruler of God's creation."*

REVELATION 3:14

Typically when we see the word *amen* we think of the closing of a prayer—a type of agreement simply meaning, *May it be so.* But here in our passage today we see the only time in Scripture where the word is used as a name for Christ. Indeed, He was the final seal, the Amen, of God's promise to mankind. Through Him the purposes of God were established.

As Jesus hung on the cross and said, "It is finished," the final sacrifice was made on our behalf. Our debt of sin was paid in full. Nothing can be added to the cross. We don't need to try to earn what Jesus already paid for, and we don't need to worry that it was not enough. There is no condemnation for those who are in Christ Jesus, for His blood has purified us from all sin. *AMEN!*

*He...*

# Stands at the Door

*I stand at the door and knock. If anyone hears
my voice and opens the door, I will come in and
eat with that person, and they with me.*

REVELATION 3:20

The door is closed. Jesus stands and knocks, waiting for His voice to be heard and the door to be opened. The Laodiceans had acquired wealth and felt as though they didn't need anything. They had grown self-sufficient, depending on their wealth rather than on God. They were lukewarm in their love for God. Apparently the door to their hearts had been open at one time, but now they didn't even hear His voice.

Why did Jesus want to come in? Was His purpose to hurt or steal or punish? No, He wanted to come in and abide; to eat together and live life together. The Laodiceans had grown lukewarm in their Christian lives because of their self-sufficient, self-centered attitudes. Hot water and cold water are both useful, but lukewarm water is distasteful! If we want to be useful, we must open the door of our hearts and dwell with Him.

# Lion of Judah

*See, the Lion of the tribe of Judah,*
*the Root of David, has triumphed.*

REVELATION 5:5

Lions are known as the king of the jungle for their majesty, authority, and power. Jesus is the Lion of the tribe of Judah. In Genesis we read the blessing Jacob gave to each of his children. To Judah he said, "You are a lion's cub, Judah...Like a lion he crouches and lies down, like a lioness—who dares to rouse him? The scepter will not depart from Judah...until he to whom it belongs shall come and the obedience of the nations shall be his."[94]

Jesus was the fulfillment of this prophecy. He is from the tribe of Judah and the lineage of David. Jesus is not only the Lamb of God—He is also the Lion of Judah, showing that He is a majestic and fierce authority as well as our humble sacrifice. I'm reminded of how C.S. Lewis describes Aslan the lion in the Chronicles of Narnia: "He isn't safe. But He is good. He is the king."[95]

*He Is the...*

# Beginning and the End

*I am the Alpha and the Omega...*
*the Beginning and the End.*
REVELATION 22:13

God has always been and always will be. He is before all things, and in Him all things hold together. *Alpha* and *omega* are the first and last letters of the Greek alphabet, an expression signifying that He is the author, the creator, and the finisher. Just as the alpha and omega stand as the bookends on either end of the Greek alphabet, so the Lord God stands on both sides of history. He is the one who holds all of history together, and He is the one who holds our story together. Our life story is meaningless without Him.

In Revelation we read that the four living beings around God's throne continually proclaim, "Holy, holy, holy is the Lord God Almighty, who was, and is, and is to come." May this be our continual proclamation as well. Let us not only honor Him in what we say... but in how we live each day as we honor the one who is Alpha and Omega, the Beginning and the End.

# Bright and Morning Star

*I am the Root and the Offspring of David,
and the bright Morning Star.*

REVELATION 22:16

The morning star is usually the brightest object in the night sky other than the moon and can be observed in the eastern sky just before the break of dawn. It is considered a symbol of hope because the darkness will soon be gone, giving way to the light of day. Jesus is our bright Morning Star, the One who has broken through the darkness of our heart with the light of God's love. He is our source of hope, because we know that one day we will no longer live in the darkness of this world, but in the light of eternity.

In the Old Testament we read the prophecy, "A star will come out of Jacob; a scepter will rise out of Israel."[96] It is believed that this is the prophecy that led the Magi to travel in search of the Messiah. Peter referred to Jesus as the morning star, writing of the time when "the day dawns and the morning star rises in your hearts."[97] May He shine brightly through you!

# Notes

1. Jeremiah 9:23-24.
2. Genesis 6:9 NLT.
3. Colossians 2:6.
4. Genesis 6:5 NLT.
5. I recommend Randy Alcorn's book *If God is Good: Faith in the Midst of Suffering and Evil* (Multnomah Publishers).
6. 1 Corinthians 10:13.
7. Jeremiah 7:12.
8. A.W. Tozer, *The Knowledge of the Holy* (New York: Harper One, 1961), 25.
9. Ephesians 1:7.
10. Psalm 48:10.
11. Psalm 89:13.
12. Psalm 44:3.
13. Isaiah 41:13.
14. http://www.spurgeon.org/sermons/0502.htm.
15. Isaiah 6:1-5.
16. Tozer, 103.
17. Colossians 1:22.
18. Colossians 3:15.
19. Deuteronomy 6:4.
20. Romans 12:19-21.
21. John 7:11.
22. Philippians 4:7.
23. Psalm 30:5.
24. Matthew 26:53.
25. 2 Chronicles 32:7-8.
26. Read the entire story in 2 Samuel 15–18.
27. Romans 11:33.
28. Romans 12:19.
29. Psalm 119:18.
30. *Streams in the Desert*, L.B. Cowman, ed. (Grand Rapids, MI: Zondervan, 1997), 188.
31. Isaiah 40:11.
32. Psalm 29:5.
33. 2 Chronicles 7:14.
34. Psalm 34:16.
35. Psalm 80:3.
36. Hebrews 4:16.
37. Isaiah 40:28-31.
38. Proverbs 3:34.
39. Luke 1:30.
40. Psalm 62:7 NLT.
41. Colossians 2:13.
42. Colossians 2:13-14.
43. 1 John 1:9.
44. Philippians 3:21.
45. Colossians 3:25.

46. Jeremiah 1:5.

47. Psalm 139:13-14.

48. Psalm 42:1-2.

49. Ephesians 3:17-19.

50. Romans 1:20 NLT.

51. Psalm 37:24.

52. Colossians 3:3.

53. John 10:28.

54. Ephesians 1:12-13.

55. Jonah 2:1-2.

56. Psalm 34:16.

57. Proverbs 11:1.

58. Psalm 19:12.

59. Matthew 13:15 NLT.

60. John 16:33 ASV.

61. Luke 2:14 ASV.

62. Romans 5:1 ASV.

63. Isaiah 61:10.

64. Matthew 5:3.

65. See Philippians 2:9-11.

66. *More Gathered Gold,* John Blanchard, ed. (Hertfordshire, England: Evangelical Press, 1986), 119.

67. Philippians 3:8-11.

68. Lamentations 3:22-24.

69. Jeremiah 9:9.

70. Colossians 1:13-14.

71. John 19:7.

72. Philippians 3:10-11.

73. Genesis 28:10-15.

74. C.S. Lewis, "Miracles," in *God in the Dock,* (Grand Rapids, MI: Eerdmans Publishing, 1942), 29.

75. Romans 5:7-8.

76. Colossians 2:13.

77. Numbers 21:4-9.

78. Acts 16:31.

79. John 6:28.

80. Hebrews 11:6.

81. John 6:35.

82. Psalm 23:3 NLT.

83. Matthew 22:16.

84. Luke 5:5-11.

85. Philippians 1:6 NLT.

86. Charles H. Spurgeon, *Complete in Christ and Love's Logic* (Whitefish, MT: Kessinger Publishing, 2006) 27.

87. Psalm 121:3.

88. Colossians 1:18.

89. Ephesians 4:15-16.

90. John 1:18.

91. Hebrews 4:15-16.

92. Colossians 2:13.

93. Luke 6:37.

94. Genesis 49:9-10.

95. C.S. Lewis, *The Lion, the Witch and the Wardrobe* (New York: Collier/Macmillan, 1970), 76.

96. Numbers 24:17.

97. 2 Peter 1:19.

## Additional Resources

If you would like an alphabetical listing of the attributes of God from this devotional, visit the author's website at KarolLadd.com for a free download. You will also find weekly uplifting messages as well as more information about Karol.

## About the Author

Karol Ladd is known as "the Positive Lady." Her heart's desire is to inspire and encourage women with a message of lasting hope and biblical truth. She is open, honest, and real in both her speaking and her writing. Formerly a teacher, Karol is the bestselling author of more than 25 books, including *A Woman's Passionate Pursuit of God, The Power of a Positive Mom,* and *The Power of a Positive Woman.* As a gifted communicator and dynamic leader, she is a popular speaker at women's organizations, church groups, and corporate events across the nation. Karol is a frequent guest on radio and television programs. Her most valued role is that of wife to Curt and mother to daughters Grace and Joy. Find more information about Karol at:

**Website:**
www.KarolLadd.com

**Blog:**
www.ThriveDontSimplySurvive.wordpress.com

**Twitter:** karolladd

**Facebook:** Karol Ladd

*Also by Karol Ladd*

**A Woman's Passionate Pursuit of God (book and DVD)**
*Creating a Positive and Purposeful Life*

As you explore Paul's intriguing letter to the Philippians with popular author and speaker Karol Ladd, you'll learn to live intentionally as you face life's daily challenges. Most important, you'll be helped to understand God's Word and His plans for your life and say more and more, "Father, I want what You want."

Filled with inspiring true-life stories, practical steps, and study questions, this book is perfect for personal quiet times, a book club pick, or a group Bible study.

It's complemented by the DVD version, offering six 30-minute sessions from Karol, a helpful leader's guide, and discussion questions. *Excellent for small-group or church class study.*

**A Woman's Secret for Confident Living (book and DVD)**
*Becoming Who God Made You to Be*

Bestselling author Karol Ladd shares powerful truths from the book of Colossians to help you make a vital shift in perspective. Knowing Christ and His greatness, and knowing who you are in Him, sets you on an exciting path to living—not in self-confidence, but *God*-confidence. You'll be helped to

- get rid of negative and self-defeating thoughts
- cultivate your potential, because you're valuable to Him
- shine with joy and assurance of what you bring to the world

*Includes questions to bring depth and dimension to individual or group study.*

In the DVD version, Karol digs transforming truth out of the Scriptures in six positive, inspiring sessions such as "Transform Your Thinking," "Grow in Christ," and "Strengthen Your Relationships." *Helpful leader's guide included for group use.*